Transatlant

Transatlantic at Last

Helen Tew

First published in the UK by:
Seafarer Books
102 Redwald Road
Rendlesham
Woodbridge
Suffolk IP12 2TE

UK ISBN   0 9542750 7 1

British Library Cataloguing in Publication Data

Tew, Helen
    Transatlantic at last
    1.Tew, Helen – travel 2.Women sailors – Biography
    3.Yachting
    I.Title
    797.1 `246`092

    ISBN 0954275071

Cover design by Louis Mackay
Typesetting and design by Julie Rainford

Photographs from Tew family archive
Maps by Claire Kennedy
Drawings by Camilla Tew

Printed in Finland by WS Bookwell OY

Many thanks to all my sons who've been so supportive, especially the wives Lucy and Emma who lent me Donald and James – and Ian who got me writing. Also to Rodger Witt for editing the text, Claire Kennedy who helped organise me and dealt with the research, photos and maps, and my grand-daughter Camilla for the line drawings; finally to Donald of course – the only reason I could have done the big trip, Edward who was "mission control" at home, and to my dear John who designed our beautiful ship for us.

CONTENTS

LIST OF MAPS

FOREWORD

With a little bit of help and invention sailing is a sport that may be indulged throughout a long life. We are still learning as we get older, and our experience is always increasing. Certainly the physical demands get harder, but can be overcome with greater determination and although we may not be as strong and fit as we were there are always ways of making a heavy task lighter. Like so many sports, it all comes down to a mental attitude. For many, advancing age appears as a psychological barrier to continuing to sail but nothing need stand in the way if you are determined, as Helen Tew showed so effectively.

This is a lovely story and a love story. Not just human love, but the love for a boat built in youth, part sold, neglected, but then restored to achieve a youthful ambition more than 70 years on. How strong the desire to cross the Atlantic must have been to the young Helen Graham for her to hold onto the dream until its fulfilment in her ninth decade. How appropriate that when she did fulfil it, it was in the boat she and her husband had built together in the early years of their marriage and which was, by this time, 64 years old.

But what is so nice is the way she has managed to put the story together, right from the very beginning, in such an enjoyable and easy read.

I have known of Helen Tew for nearly 50 years. Her son Donald and I briefly served together on a Merchant Navy cadetship. However I did not meet her until after she had completed her remarkable voyage. Typically she tries to claim that it is not remarkable, but she forgets how many people close to 90 years of age would never dream of such a voyage and would assuage any doubts by claiming that at their age such a voyage was irresponsible. They are wrong, she is so right and she is a wonderful example to us all of how to get the most out of our lives and not allow fashion, custom, "expert's" advice, or age to stand in the way if we really want to do something. When young people achieve something great we always ask what they will do next. It is not often that one says the same to a nonagenarian, but having read this manuscript I would not put anything past her. Well done Helen, and thank you for making me wonder what I should do when I reach 90!

Robin Knox-Johnston

PROLOGUE

"Land!"

I staggered up on deck, still half-asleep and saw Donald pointing towards the horizon.

"That's Antigua, Mum," he said. I could hardly believe it. We'd made it – after averaging about 100 miles a day for 27 days. Pretty good for a little old boat – not to mention a little old lady! Naturally, I felt triumphant – but I had no idea that my cruise across the pond would cause such a stir. I returned to find myself the subject of articles in newspapers and magazines all over the world.

"A voyage of remarkable courage, sheer bloody-mindedness and no small measure of score settling," is the way Stewart Payne described it in *The Daily Telegraph.*

The Times ran a full length article about a 'white-haired and disarming' old woman who didn't suffer fools gladly. As I told their reporter, "When someone asked me how I was getting back to England, I said 'sail of course'. Silly ass".

The Daily Mirror was more prosaic. "A gran of 89 yesterday became the oldest woman to cross the Atlantic and back in a small boat," it told its readers.

All this was most unexpected and hard to fathom. Compared to the exploits of, say, Ellen MacArthur, Tracy Edwards or Clare Francis, my two-way trip was simply an afternoon sail. But, for some reason, people seemed genuinely interested – inspired even. Above all, they wondered, why, in heaven's name, would someone of my age decide to do something like this? My reply was always the same: why not?

You see, I never felt old. It was only when I looked in my passport and saw my date of birth that I gave it any thought.

Not only that, I'd always wanted to sail the Atlantic. When I was only a child, my father, Cdr Douglas Graham, promised that, one day, we would do the trip together – but in 1934, he went without me. He even wrote a book about it called *Rough Passage* – now something of a classic – which, I'm afraid, I refused to read. I was terribly upset and felt a huge sense of disappointment. Shortly afterwards, there was talk of the family cruising to Canada but war intervened so, once again, it all came to nothing.

By that time, I was married and starting a family. Eventually, with five boys (Donald, Ian, Edward, Malcolm and James) to bring up, I was simply too busy to do anything about it.

In fact, I had to wait until the end of the millennium before my chance came again.

By then though, the odds seemed slim. I was in my eighty-ninth year, and our little boat, *Mary Helen*, designed by my naval architect husband John, was a mature sixty-four, and laid up in Dartmouth.

John died in 1975 and finding enough money to keep her in a reasonable state of repair had been something of a struggle. Not surprisingly therefore, she looked sad and unloved. It was all rather depressing.

Finally, the young man working at the yard in Mill Creek said he would take her off our hands and do her up at his own expense. In the end, we came to a compromise, which meant I at least kept a share in her, and he promptly started work.

The trouble was, he then decided to get married, and consequently had less time to spare, so poor *Mary Helen* began to look neglected again.

To make matters worse, my home on the banks of the Solent was threatened by coastal erosion and flooding. It would cost a great deal to put things right. At that moment I seemed to have taken a couple of steps backwards. Apart from anything else, where on earth would the money come from?

Our only option was to sell a modest bungalow on our small estate. Luckily, we got a good price for it and we actually ended up with a surplus. That was all the incentive I needed, which is why I asked Edward, my financial son, whether I could afford to get *Mary Helen* back.

When he assured me I could, there was no stopping me. As far as I was concerned, the adventure had already begun.

Chapter One

ROMANCE AND (ALMOST) DISASTER

Fantastic; *Mary Helen* was mine again! She needed a considerable amount of work, including a new deck but eventually, everything was finished and Edward, his eldest daughter Camilla, and I clambered aboard her at Dartmouth in the West Country and proudly hoisted the Royal Cruising Club (R.C.C.) burgee.

It was an emotional moment because it brought back memories of the day she was first launched in April 1937. It also reminded me of my husband John who designed her. He made his first sketch of our little boat on the back of a menu in a hotel in Fowey when we were on our honeymoon. But that was a long time ago.

I first caught sight of this handsome young man in Lymington in 1935. Had I not sat on my father's binoculars and broken them I would never have been there at all.

I'd been sailing *Emanuel*, the family boat on my own at the time and was so worried when the accident happened that, after picking up our mooring in the Beaulieu River, I jumped on my bicycle and pedalled into Lymington to get them repaired. Whether I did or not, I honestly can't remember. But I do recall deciding to look for a replacement tender at Berthon's Boat Yard because the dinghy Dad brought back from Bermuda was horrid, flat and unstable. I didn't get a tender; I found a husband instead.

I had no idea who John Tew was at the time, of course, I simply noticed him talking to one of the workers in the yard.

Not sure what to do next, I remembered that Lymington was the home of Jack Laurent Giles the famous yacht designer. Could someone there tell me whether I could get my father's boat measured, so we could race her, I wondered? That might be fun.

So, feeling brave, I made my way to 4 Quay Hill and, to my surprise, was greeted by the same charming chap I'd seen in the yard.

"What can I do for you?"

"I wondered about getting a yacht measured for the Royal Ocean Racing Club."

"And what yacht would that be?"

"She's called *Emanuel*".

He smiled. "Are you Helen Graham?"

I nodded.

"I know all about you," he said, and promptly invited me to tea at the Royal Lymington Yacht Club.

In those days, the lounge was downstairs and you rang a bell for the steward.

"Tea for two, please, Francis," said John – and that, I suppose, was the start of our courtship. Afterwards John Tew drove me back to Ginn's Farm on the banks of the Beaulieu River with my bike in the back of his Riley. We married the following July.

That first summer was bliss. John came sailing in *Emanuel* and I crewed for him in his Montague Sharpie racing dinghy. We nearly capsized once and John was teased for looking at his girlfriend rather than where he was going. We sailed, and laughed – and danced the night away at The Royal Lymington Yacht Club Regatta Ball.

In term time I was Miss Graham, the maths mistress at Leeson House in Swanage.

John would meet me on my afternoon off and take me for tea at Studland. I can still remember the black cherry jam; once tasted, never forgotten.

Everything was going so well, until the autumn, when we had a terrible storm in Poole Harbour. It was during the holidays and I was spending some time on board alone – which was perfectly normal, though on this occasion the weather was anything but. We were on a mooring opposite Hamworthy and I'd finished eating my supper and turned in. Not long afterwards I was shaken from my slumbers by a violent bucking motion so I went on deck to investigate. Steadying myself against the fearsome wind I noticed a yacht drifting past with no one at the helm – and then another. Clearly, having broken free from their moorings, they were drifting out of control. I clambered forward to check that all was OK – but saw straight away that *Emanuel* was dragging and realised that something had to be done. Somehow, I managed to get the anchor out – which seemed to stop her – but was worried it might not be enough so brought the kedge up, bent on another warp, and hurled it over the side. The boat was still pitching ferociously but at least we weren't moving. In my sopping wet pyjamas, I paused to take stock and, after deciding there was nothing more I could do, went back below. I dried myself, got dressed and then spent the rest of the night popping up and down to make sure we stayed put.

Some time later, a friend asked me why I remained with the boat rather than going ashore in the tender. In all honesty, I simply never thought about it – and anyway, you never leave your ship unless she's sinking. On the other hand, I must say how pleased I was next morning to see John, my new boyfriend, rowing out to meet me. Obviously concerned about my safety, he said it would be silly to spend another night afloat so, once back on dry land, we called up my friends, the Hultons, who lived locally, and they kindly offered to put me up.

After John left I remember Colonel Hulton looking at me with a twinkle in his eye.

"He'll do, Helen," he said, "He'll do!"

According to a report at the time in the *Poole & East Dorset Herald*, The Great Storm, as they described it, was probably the worst in local history with about a hundred boats blown from their moorings, some tossed on to the promenade and one ending up in someone's front garden. Trees were uprooted, the lifeboat ran aground – as did thirty yachts, five of which sank – and a spring tide flooded the streets.

Having survived all that, it was ironic that *Emanuel* should be sunk some time later, not by high winds but by ice. Water which had frozen along the marshy edges of the Wareham Channel had floated off in sheets on the tide and slid menacingly down the Harbour. These dangerously jagged shards had sawn away at *Emanuel*'s bows and made a fateful gash. After she was hauled out we asked John to conduct a survey.

He arrived later with the awful news and even showed me a tiny part of one of *Emanuel*'s frames – all decomposed and powdery. It was in a matchbox, like someone's ashes and I remember being so upset and angry that I nearly decided to have nothing more to do with him.

Poor *Emanuel*; she was eventually repaired but Dad sold her shortly afterwards – which only made matters worse. This boat was part of my life. I think the new owner finally understood what was going on.

"You don't like me very much, do you?" he asked.

"To be perfectly honest, no I don't," I replied rather ungraciously.

With *Emanuel* gone, in the Easter holidays I went sailing in a boat called *Herga*.

My mother was unenthusiastic because I was the only girl amongst six men; even John was dubious. But I assured them there was safety in numbers.

It was then that John fixed a date to buy an engagement ring.

After the wedding I was busy until the end of term – but in August we were lent a little boat called *Kishti* for our honeymoon. This was the first time I'd sailed a boat with an engine and we meandered gently down to Dartmouth and the West Country.

As I say, it was in Fowey that John made the first rough sketches of a pretty little 26-footer. We were enjoying a slap-up meal in the Grand Hotel overlooking the harbour at the time and were so taken with the idea that we decided to go and see Percy Mitchell to find out how much such a boat might cost to build.

Percy who owned a yard in Mevagissey said he could offer us a six tonner for £200 or a nine tonner for £250. Since there was no way we could afford the extra £50, it was six tons or nothing and the deal was done.

Incidentally, just in case you were wondering, when referring to the size of a boat, builders nearly always used 'tons' to indicate how big she was. But, of course, these were 'Thames' tons, and had nothing to do with weight. Thames Measurement, which had been around since 1855, was really a rough way of calculating volume using a boat's length and beam. End of history lesson!

As it happened, I always vowed to marry someone with a boat. John didn't have a boat – but at least he promised to build me one!

That autumn, we spent many hours completing the final design. While John worked on the drawings I clicked away with the knitting needles and offered helpful suggestions. At least, I hope they were; he never said they weren't.

Eventually, we ended up with a beautiful, long-keeled six ton gaff cutter. She measured 26.4ft overall and 23.4ft on the waterline, with 8.2ft beam, 4.7ft draft and 462 sq ft of sail.

At the same time, Jack Laurent Giles had been asked by a chap called Dick Kinnersley to design a five tonner for serious offshore cruising. The result, a 25-footer called *Andrillot*, was the forerunner of the famous Vertue class which were built in large numbers and eventually criss-crossed the globe. As you might expect, there were similarities between our boat and Jack's but I always maintain that the famous Giles sheer-strake, which became something of a signature, was actually influenced by my John. It was his idea.

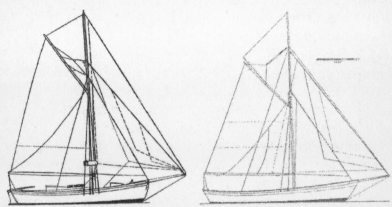

Spot the difference: *Mary Helen* on the left and *Andrillot* on the right.
Our boat is slightly larger, but the family likeness is unmistakable.
Mary Helen drawn by John Tew,
Andrillot drawing courtesy Jack Laurent Giles.

Every available weekend we travelled to Mevagissey to watch our dream ship take shape. We stayed in the local bed and breakfast run by Bessie Martin who seemed almost as excited as we were.

At last *Mary Helen* was ready. She would be launched in April 1937.

When the great day arrived, the conditions were far from ideal. Percy Mitchell later admitted that his instinct had been to wait until the weather improved – but we were so enthusiastic, and obviously eager to get on with it, he agreed to press ahead.

In those days, they had to move the boat down on to the sands at low water and leave her there until she floated off with the tide. By lunch time, with our smart new boat propped up in the middle of the dried out bay, we went into town for some last minute shopping.

A few hours later we returned, expecting to see her afloat. But as we rounded the bend in the road we realised that something was wrong. For a start, there were lots of people standing around.

Then we saw her. She was lying on her side with the waves breaking over her. Water was sluicing in through the cabin and out through the forehatch. As Percy later wrote in his book *A Boat Builder's Story*, 'Mrs Tew cried'. I certainly did. After all our efforts, to see her like that was simply heartbreaking. It showed just how dangerous launching on an open beach can be – particularly in high winds and choppy seas.

As a result of our misfortune however Percy eventually got permission to knock a gap in the wall which meant that subsequently, at high water, boats could be launched properly on a slipway. So some good came out of it.

Back in 1937 though, there was nothing anyone could do until the tide receded, which meant waiting around until dark. To help us see what was going on, the owner of a baby Austin car kindly ran his engine and switched on the headlamps. Finally, a number of helpers manhandled her up the beach and back into the yard.

Oh dear! What a sorry sight. It was all most distressing, so, feeling helpless – we returned to the bed and breakfast for another night. Even Bessie burst into tears.

There was only one bright spot in all of this. John had insured her half an hour before the launch.

Next morning, John and Percy surveyed the damage. It was bad, but Percy thought he could patch her up. A couple of months later, *Mary Helen* was afloat and ready for sea.

In spite of her modest proportions, I found her incredibly roomy. That's because of her raised deck – something I was used to on our previous boats. It's a far more practical arrangement than a conventional coachroof, in my view, and undoubtedly increases the space down below. The foc'sle still has a pipe cot to port, as it did then, and a fixed berth to starboard. The galley aft was a primus stove in gimbals, to port, with a wet locker opposite. When the wind died we called on the trusty eight horsepower Stuart Turner two-stroke which lived beneath the bridgedeck. It would only be used as a last resort, or preferably not at all, if I had my way, – which, perhaps, is why John said I developed what he called my 'motoring look' whenever we used it.

Sadly, on this occasion, John had been ill and was still recovering, so, for her maiden voyage, I sailed her back to Poole with my father. We hardly touched the helm. With the wind just east of north she happily steered herself.

Naturally, I was absolutely thrilled with her; as a matter of fact, I still am.

Now, here we were, all those years later, sailing her home again – not to Poole this time, but back to the Solent. She felt as good as new.

We had a super sail up Channel. The sun shone, and at times, *Mary Helen* scampered along at 7 knots. We spent a night in Weymouth then came in past the Needles and finally fetched up in the beautiful Beaulieu River.

So far so good!

Chapter Two

SECRET DESTINATION

With *Mary Helen* back in commission we took part in the September 1999 Royal Cruising Club rally – sailing back through the fleet, resplendent under full canvas, including the topsail. We'd also intended to take part in their rolling meet the following spring but told anyone who asked that we might be sailing south instead.

We knew what we meant, even if they didn't. Still, we managed to rendezvous with everyone at the Jersey meet and came back via Dilette and Guernsey. We had a super send off from St Peter Port with Donald's staff cheering and waving from the windows of his office which overlooks the harbour.

Back home again, full of confidence, I started planning. In my little bungalow, which is virtually on the beach, I began making lists. Because hardly anyone outside the family knew what I was up to, it was like a secret operation – but with good reason. So many people talk big but then don't follow through, or only get as far as Vigo in Spain, that I saw no point in raising expectations.

The family were understanding and also extremely supportive; I remember shopping for supplies in Winchester with Lucy my daughter in law, who had a habit of doubling up the quantities I'd asked for. It was all for the best possible motives of course – and I don't know what I would have done without her. I also bought some new oilies; a far cry from the sort of things I wore as a girl. In those days females were expected to wear skirts and look ladylike – it seems unimaginable now.

Donald also bought some new charts. Some of the ones I had were pretty antique and dated back to my father's days in the navy.

I've since been asked whether I was apprehensive but I wasn't. It was my life-long ambition – and, after all, I had confidence in the boat, and was getting one over on Dad.

This time too, we would have modern electronic navigational equipment. There was no such thing as GPS when *Mary Helen* was launched; we relied on more traditional methods to plot our position. Perhaps that's why I felt so relaxed about the whole thing, and anyway, we had a sextant and tables with us just in case something went wrong with the electronics.

I was used to cruising in small boats and had served my apprenticeship.

I've also never lived far from the sea; it's always been part of my life. Indeed, my earliest memory was a picnic at Burnham-on-Sea. That would have been in 1916 when I was only four; we went in a pony and trap.

"Where's the sea?" I asked indignantly when we arrived.

"Over there," said my mother pointing across the sands to a darker line in the distance. I quickly donned a pair of 'paddlers' – revolting yellow oilskin pants – and though it looked a long way away, set off to find it. Alas, the tide was out – you have very high tides in the Bristol Channel – and the dark line was Burnham mud. After managing a few steps, I fell flat on my face in the soft, sticky gunge and had to be scrubbed and cleaned. My mother was most unhappy about it.

I was actually born in sunny Southsea in Hampshire, the first of four children, in 1912. As Leonard Wesson recently reminded me on a thoughtful birthday card, it was quite a year.

'RMS *Titanic* sailed from Southampton on her ill-fated maiden voyage bound for New York, Captain Robert Scott discovered that Amundsen had already reached the South Pole, Ballets Russes performed Ravel's, Daphnis and Chloe, Hobbs and Rhodes scored a first wicket partnership of 323 in the Melbourne Test, Oxford refloated after sinking and won the Boat Race, telephones were nationalised, tophats were abolished at Rugby School, Thomas Hardy was 72, satin bathing suits became popular and, of course, Helen arrived!'

My father was a sub-lieutenant in the Navy at the time – and eventually ended up as Commander. However, when he inherited a fruit farm in 1915, we moved to Somerset.

To begin with, since my father had no boat of his own, he sailed with a chap called Klugh. In all honesty, my father's early sailing exploits were less than auspicious.

His first attempt to cross the Bristol Channel in a dinghy ended in ignominious failure – and he had to be rescued. He didn't get very far. After the dinghy incident, his first proper yacht – a five ton gaff cutter called *Vixen* was lost in the North Sea.

Apparently, after a Chinese gybe (in which the gaff and the boom swing across the boat in opposite directions) she was taken in tow but was dragged along too quickly and subsequently foundered.

During the Great War, as you might expect, he was kept extremely busy in the Navy and, rather momentously, was an officer on the last trans-Pacific Naval ship with sails. In those days there was simply no way they could carry enough coal to cover that sort of distance.

Dad used to say that his horticultural interest began here when he started growing cucumbers up the rigging! As I shall explain later, when he retired he took up fruit farming in Somerset.

Anyway, when the armistice came in 1918, I remember being given a flag and told to go and tell granny – who, having been evacuated from London, was living in the village. I had no idea what it was all about though I realised it must be important and something worth celebrating.

By that time, I was at boarding school. In fact I was only seven when I first went away. That's because it was about eleven miles to the nearest suitable school and, without cars, was quite a round trip in a pony and trap.

Then, in 1923, my father asked me a most important question.

"Would you like to come sailing with me, Helen?"

At my mother's suggestion, he'd chartered a four tonner called *Irish Molly*.

Of course, I said yes. Apart from anything else, it sounded like a great adventure, although I had no clear idea of what a yacht might actually look like. After a brief explanation, I gathered it had a cabin, so I imagined it would probably resemble an open boat, like the ones used by local fishermen, but with some sort of house perched in the middle.

Anyhow, Dad went on ahead to check everything out; I was to join him later at Burnham-on-Crouch. Getting there from Groombridge meant taking a train; my first journey by rail! I felt extremely grown up and proudly informed my travelling companions that I was going 'yachting'. They smiled politely but said nothing.

Dad met me at the station and in no time we were in a dinghy making our way out to a small white boat in the distance. I was too overawed by everything to ask about the cabin but felt sure that Dad knew where everything was.

As I clambered on board I grabbed hold of the boom which swung across the boat and almost pitched me over the side. What followed was my first lesson.

"Now, Helen, remember, if you fall overboard you'll drown."

It was a maxim I've remembered ever since and often repeated to my children.

As for the sailing itself, we had plenty of bad weather. Reading my father's log now, I realise I must have been pretty tough. Neither strong headwinds nor seasickness seem to have put me off. Above all, I remember having fun.

I was also thrilled by the sight of porpoises darting around us, and herons on the river bank, not to mention teas in restaurants and even dinner in a hotel.

One night, the boat dried out and at low water was heeling over at a most acute angle. I turned in on the lower or leeward side and remember waking up and exclaiming, "Oh Daddy, I'm sleeping in water!" In fact, it was true because as the tide came in, the topsides started to leak and the boat had begun to fill.

I had no idea at the time but it seems Dad had a lot of bailing to do and was worried that she might not refloat. Luckily, everything turned out OK apart from a lot of wet clothes – which, as I've since discovered is perfectly normal on a boat.

The following year we had another four tonner. Dad was in Penarth taking part in a chess championship when he chanced upon Anderson's modest yard and saw this most attractive little boat called *Onaway* which he decided to charter. This time, he took my younger brother John as well. I remember Mum driving us over to Burnham and having a picnic on the sands and waiting for the tide to come in. By the time there was enough water, the wind had got up and Dad had to take us out in the dinghy, one by one. It was really rough and I thought we might sink.

It wasn't much better on board. *Onaway* was rolling like a pig, so John and I were mighty pleased when Dad gave up the idea of sailing to Minehead and ran up-river instead. Our reprieve was short-lived though. At 0400 on August 2nd, having been summoned from our bunks, we were beating back the other way. It was horrible. John was seasick, I felt ill and even Dad looked green. Not surprisingly, no one wanted any breakfast.

We had a pretty lively sail towards Minehead but had to anchor off Greenhaly Point to wait for enough water to enter the harbour. At last, everything was calm and quiet. We even managed to eat something.

Food always makes you feel better, so we decided to row down to the sands and have a game of cowboys and indians or cops and robbers. But when we got there, Dad said it was too rough to land; the spoilsport. I was peeved, so when we got back to *Onaway*, ignoring all sensible advice, I went for a swim. The water was freezing.

High water was still in the early hours of the morning, so we were woken up at 0330.

It took a couple of hours to unship the legs – which were used to stop the boat falling over when she dried out – and get ready for sea. Again it was too early for breakfast and once out in the open sea, the motion was so lively that food was the last thing on our minds. However, I wouldn't admit to feeling sick.

"I'm just not hungry." I told Dad.

We reached Oxwich Bay at 1115 and anchored. The boat was still rolling, so we went ashore for a picnic. Once on dry land, our appetites miraculously returned.

Returning to *Onaway*, we rigged her for heavy weather and weighed anchor. Beyond the Point, the sea was nasty and rough. When Dad decided to go back, John and I had no complaints.

We were underway again the following morning after breakfast because the tide was that much later. With a light, westerly wind we had to beat, and made slow progress even with the topsail set. Without the ebb tide, we would have probably been sailing backwards. Eventually, through the drizzle and mist, we spotted land. It was a beacon marking the entrance to Tenby. Dad had hoped to make Caldy Island but the tide was on the turn so we anchored off the pier at 1400.

As a treat, we rowed ashore for tea, but when we went back to the pier they charged us 4d a head. Dad was outraged. "A shilling is an undue tax for an hour ashore," he wrote in the log. (Note to younger readers – that's 5p in today's money.)

To make us all feel better John cooked 'a satisfying supper of fried mushrooms', after which we weighed anchor and beat through Caldy Sound. John and I turned in at about 2230 and slept like babies. We woke to find Dad had been sailing the boat by himself and had reached Milford Haven.

The next few days were spent exploring the area. The weather was far from ideal and on one occasion, Dad wrote 'John, sitting in the bows, had rather a bad time – but as he was wet already, it didn't matter'. John was less stoic, even when his father assured him he was acting like a breakwater and helping to keep the rest of us dry.

We sailed to Skomar the following day. It was flat calm to begin with but the wind steadily increased, so did the rain which was torrential by the time we anchored in North Haven. It's a fascinating island with masses of puffins and gulls perched on the cliffs. They seemed so tame, you felt you could pick them up.

Dad was less concerned about the wildlife and more worried about a change in the weather. In those days, getting trapped on a lee shore was a genuine worry because few boats had engines. Things are easier now in some ways, though skippers still have their problems – not least the growth of conservation issues and petty bureaucracy. I doubt now whether we would be allowed to anchor in some of the places we visited back in the twenties.

At about 1200 the following day, we set off in fine weather and a light south-westerly wind bound for Ireland. We passed the Bishop Rock and several light ships, and watched the Welsh coast gently fade away as we steered our little ship beneath the stars. By morning, the wind had dropped, and Wicklow came into view.

We finished the last of the bread at breakfast; the rest of our stores were running low too, so John and I were keen to get ashore. Dad agreed, so we anchored in Wicklow Bay at noon. We filled some old petrol cans with water which Dad said would be fine but I never got used to the taste.

As the wind got up, the boat started to roll again so we decided to move, and sailed to the inner harbour where we tied up alongside the pier. John and I rowed ashore and had fun paddling about in a rocky cove. Since there were plenty of people around, I was too shy to bathe.

Our passage to the Isle of Man was extremely rough and we were soaked when we finally reached Peel. Luckily neither of us felt seasick and it all seemed rather exciting. The only boring bit was cleaning up the boat afterwards and hanging out all our wet clothes in the rigging.

Dad never wasted too much time in harbour if he could help it, so the next day we set off for Ireland again.

After about eighteen hours, we reached Strangford Loch. There's a famous whirlpool in the entrance called the Routen Wheel and John and I were quite looking forward to seeing it. In the event, it seemed pretty tame, though Dad said it might be dangerous in bad weather, particularly for someone in a dinghy.

He also told us that Scotland was off the agenda and that, after a day or so exploring Strangford Loch we would sail south for home.

That suited us fine. We met up with a couple of friends and took them for a sail – which meant the boat was rather crowded – and I remember the problem we had weighing the anchor which was solid with weed.

On another occasion I dropped the parallel rulers over the side. Dad never shouted, but simply said "Oh Helen" in a disappointed sort of way – which was worse.

When the wind dropped, John and I took turns towing the boat in the dinghy – which was hard work but thoroughly enjoyable. Messing about like this was brilliant – particularly after having to get up at unearthly hours to catch the tide.

I remember catching lobsters and crabs and boiling them in a bucket balanced on a Primus in the cockpit. It was probably indescribably dangerous but the food tasted wonderful.

Through all this, we were learning and getting used to life afloat. As Dad recorded in his log, 'Both children are pretty well trained now.' As a case in point, when it was time to leave, we were underway in five minutes.

When we finally reached Ireland, we weren't precisely sure which side of the border we were on since partition had only recently taken place. Incidentally, in those days, the IRA was still a relatively recent phenomenon, and had only been operating as an underground paramilitary organisation since its clash with Irish government forces in 1922. Our concern, however, was more geographical than political, so to solve the dilemma, Dad rowed ashore and, instead of asking someone, called at the local post office and bought a penny stamp.

Problem solved.

It took us three days to get from Carlingford to Burnham, some 239 miles, in extremely mixed conditions. It certainly blew hard when we went ashore because I remember getting wet as I clambered out of the dinghy and fell over.

There were several people watching and one old man said, "Grace, darling, take care, and don't be in such a hurry." Which, for some reason, made everyone laugh.

Mum refused to let me sail the last lap to Penarth because she said I needed to get back and buy some new clothes for school. What a pain!

Eventually though, one summer we did indeed manage to make it to Scotland in spite of some pretty foul weather. We called in at Peel again and visited the castle by the harbour – and I particularly remember visiting Bangor and buying a cotton frock for eight shillings. It was yellow with black spots. Back at school after the holidays we were told to write an essay about our summer holidays. Naturally I described our cruise. When our homework was returned, mine had a large red cross by the word 'Bangor' with the footnote *Bangor is in Wales*. I took great delight in retorting, "Yes, Miss Lloyd Thomas but there's one in Ireland too!" To rub it in, I even showed her on the map.

As I say, the climax of that cruise was reaching Scotland – which, of course, is where the Grahams originated. I felt a rush of emotion when we sailed into Lowlandman's Bay; the scenery was so different. Somerset was rural and flat; this was dramatic and mountainous. We sailed up to the head of Loch Long, then walked across to look at Loch Lomond. I enjoyed every moment of it, but halfway back, brother John stopped. Standing resolutely in the middle of the road, he stamped his foot and announced firmly, "I will not look at another view."

Actually, as things turned out, this was his last cruise with us. It was less to do with looking at views, I think, than the fact that he never really overcame his problem with seasickness. Perhaps there was one other important factor too – no doubt he wanted to spend time with his friends. Sailing with his father and sister was beginning to lose its appeal.

Our next boat was *Emanuel*, a 30 footer which Dad found in the same yard.

He simply fell in love with her – and because we'd had a good crop of apples – decided to buy her. Like *Onaway*, she had raised topsides, which made her very roomy below – and, of course, when you sat down, you didn't bang the back of your head against the side of the cabin.

During this time I was busy getting educated. I went to Cheltenham, where, I found I had an aptitude for maths. Then it was on to Bedford College, London University as one of '600 earnest females seeking after knowledge' where I decided to be a teacher.

I loved school, partly, I suppose, because I was a relatively placid child and did as I was told. Funnily enough, my sister Marguerite was the complete opposite.

She loathed it!

In the holidays, we cruised the Bristol Channel and sailed as far as Ireland, Scotland, France and Spain.

By that time, I was hooked on sailing particularly with my father – so it was immensely gratifying all these years later, to start the first leg of my grand, Atlantic adventure, not just with my son Donald, but also with my eldest grandson Michael. We were continuing a family tradition.

The three of us left the Agamemnon boatyard on the Beaulieu River on the evening of August 1st 2000. It was a fair old slog to the Beaulieu River Sailing Club pontoon at the mouth of the river – not least because it was blustery, cold and dark.

The following day saw heavy rain as well as high winds so we took time to make sure that everything was properly stowed.

We set sail the day after that in a fresh westerly breeze and set off down the Solent.

It was fairly rough outside and poor Michael succumbed to seasickness just as his grandmother had all those years ago on *Irish Molly*. There's no point bashing on if you don't have to, so we put into Studland Bay, just outside Poole Harbour, where we enjoyed a quiet and peaceful night. Thankfully, Michael quickly recovered, after which he decided it might be a good idea to take his seasickness pills!

Having sorted that one out, we enjoyed an easy passage to Lagos in Portugal.

Chapter Three

NORWAY HERE WE COME

Before leaving Lagos we spent a couple of days waiting for a weather front to pass.

With heavy rain, and strong, west-south-west winds, we thought it made sense to stay put. It also gave us a chance to restow everything and correct a slight list to starboard, as well as a tendency to trim by the stern. After a lot of hard work shifting stuff about, the boat was back on an even keel.

Then, on September 20th, 2000, after an early breakfast, we were ready for sea, and bound for Madeira, or rather Porto Santo, one of the other islands of the Archipelagos. We decided against Madeira itself because people told us that Funchal, the usual port of call, was unfriendly, crowded and uncomfortable.

After topping up the engine oil, we passed through the bridge and took on diesel.

The wind picked up from the south as we left the narrow entrance and before long, we were headed with winds which were so light, fluky and inconsistent – that we started the engine, to get us clear, then motor-sailed for the next three hours. It's not really my idea of fun – but as my old friend Claude Worth said in one of his books, 'There's no dishonour in running your engine to get to a place where you know there's some wind'. Anyway, by 1400 a more substantial breeze filled in from the north-west, so we killed the mechanical monster and soaked up the silence.

A huge swell from west-north-west, combined with a head sea, dampened our progress, although we still managed a creditable 2½ to 3½ knots.

As night fell, we cleared the shipping lanes around Cape St Vincent. The hazy cloud had moved away, uncovering a magical spread of stars above our heads – with the Milky Way shimmering like a veil. All the time, *Mary Helen* ploughed relentlessly on, carving a bright, phosphorescent path though the water. This pleasant experience continued all night, with the wind veering north-east by dawn. For a few hours, we boomed out the staysail until the wind backed to the north and gradually increased. By the time it reached Force 4, *Mary Helen* was at her best, surging along at 5½ knots. The sun was shining, the sea moderate and, give or take the odd roll or two, the motion relatively comfortable. The passage took 4 days, 22 hours and we soon settled down to a regular watch-keeping routine of four hours on, and four hours off. It was a system we stuck to, whatever happened – even if our time below was interrupted by some emergency or crisis. I took midnight to 0400, then 0800 to midday, and 1600 to 2000, whilst Donald filled in the gaps.

What you did during your time below was entirely up to you. The constant movement of the boat made reading or sewing just about impossible – so we generally slept; at least I did. Luckily, I don't have any difficulty sleeping, even on a small boat bobbing about in the ocean; I've had plenty of practice.

I even got plenty of sleep on my first cruise on *Mary Helen* in 1938 – at least I did after the first stage of the trip. John had decided to leave his job running Napier's yard at Hamworthy in Poole, and we'd set off for Norway. It was just the two of us and all the duties were equally shared. If anyone dared to call me a cook-housekeeper on board a boat I got extremely angry.

Having stored our furniture and dumped our clothes, along with the dog and her nine puppies on my long-suffering family, we were ready to go.

On 30th April, we left Poole Bar buoy and, initially, because of an easterly wind, headed west. Why make life difficult? And anyway, we'd borrowed a huge number of charts so even if we kept going, then sailed up to the Orkneys, Shetlands and Færoes, and down the North Sea, we could still reach our destination, and were adequately covered. We also had a portable three-valve Wayfarer wireless set complete with internal aerial – a really modern, state-of-the-art piece of equipment – which worked perfectly from start to finish. Our only other sophisticated piece of hardware was a barograph, which gave us accurate atmospheric pressure readings, and helped us work out what the weather was doing.

After a super sixteen and a half hour sail, well reefed down, in a brisk breeze we reached Dartmouth and turned in. According to the log, we slept until late.

We spent the next few days in harbour, finishing off all the odd jobs that would have been done in Poole – had we not been so keen to get going. As it happened, with such a strong, cold, north-easterly wind blowing, pressing on would have been a test of endurance, so, in the event, it all worked out rather well.

A few days later, we sailed down to Mevagissey where we had a cooked chicken and a leg of lamb waiting for us. It probably sounds strange now, but back then, people often arranged to have hot meals prepared at the bake house. You regularly saw them scurrying to and fro, carrying their Sunday lunches.

The following morning we set off again, under the watchful eye of Mr Chesterfield who made *Mary Helen*'s sails; admiring his handiwork, no doubt.

After a light, variable breeze, the wind freshened up from the south and we enjoyed some marvellous sailing until, of course, it got cold and wet. We then handed the main and jib, and continued under staysail alone, managing thirty-four miles in eight hours in a genuine, full-blooded Force 7 – as later confirmed by the local lighthouse keeper. The log was suitably terse: 'thick, rain, vile, cold,' it read.

Approaching the coast of Holyhead we ran into dense fog, which was bad enough.

But we had another nasty shock. We were expecting the South Stack fog signal – as described in the almanac – but heard something completely different. Eventually, we reached the North Stack mark which as the fog momentarily lifted, was plainly visible, so we knew we were right and the fog signal wrong. We were subsequently told that the signal had indeed been changed.

After four days at sea, we went ashore in our wet clothes and had a wonderful bath which, according to my log, cost an exorbitant amount of money. I also noted that the bathrooms themselves lacked privacy and would only be suitable for married couples. Intriguing; I wonder exactly what I meant?

From Holyhead, we sailed to Larne, then on to Lowlandman's Bay in Jura before reaching Oban and Little Horseshoe Bay to visit Mr Leslie the famous lobster fisherman. This last leg was an extremely pleasant beat in bright sunshine and we anchored just inside the entrance and had a walk to Gylen Castle.

Mr Leslie was pleased to see me. One of his daughters clearly remembered my last visit in *Blue Dragon*, the boat owned by skipper Lynham, headmaster of the Dragon school in Oxford, and greeted me with "Mary, Helen Graham!" – extremely flattering.

We were also presented with a couple of lobsters which was greatly appreciated.

On Monday, May 23rd, we reached Fort William where Mr McLean, the ferryman, kindly gave us four large motor tyres for the canal. They proved extremely useful.

We also did some shopping and I met an old school friend; a pleasant coincidence.

Back on the boat, we climbed 'Neptune's Staircase' at the entry to the Canal and spent the night on board. Just after breakfast the following morning, we slipped our lines and left.

The weather was fine, and, with lights twinkling on the hills, we felt happy and relaxed. With a fairy-tale view, a sound ship and time to enjoy it all, what else could anyone want?

Lunch time found us sailing peacefully in light airs through Loch Lochy with just the yankee set. It was incredibly beautiful with trees and islets all around and no one else in sight. But nothing lasts forever, and later on, it started drizzling. By the time we made fast at Fort Augustus is was raining really hard.

Our next important destination was Loch Ness. We entered, with eyes peeled, looking round in all directions but obviously on this occasion, the monster was having a day off. Without much wind, we had to motor a lot, which I normally find tiresome, but this time, running the engine had an added advantage. It provided a steady stream of hot, fresh water from the loch which gave me the opportunity to do some washing. The trouble was, I had to find gaps in the rain, so I could hang it out to dry.

Approaching Inverness, we saw a man and his small daughter wearily paddling a canoe. They looked so forlorn and bedraggled that we offered them a tow which was gratefully accepted. When we moored above the Muirtown locks they came aboard for tea.

The girl's father was an engine driver on holiday and most interesting. That's one of the pleasures of cruising; you never know who you're going to meet!

On Monday, May 30th, we passed through the last lock with a gift of milk and a lovely bunch of roses from the lockkeeper's wife. The sun shone brightly at last, and, as we sailed away under full canvas, we noticed snow on the distant hills.

On to Lossiemouth which seemed remarkably prosperous; none of the fishing boats looked more than about eight years old. Ramsay Macdonald came from these parts; perhaps that had something to do with it. Whatever the reason, the contrast with Buckie, a few miles further on, was dramatic. The fishermen there were far from happy and clearly struggling to make a living.

Then, at 1030 on Thursday, June 2nd, we heard one of the most terrifying weather forecasts imaginable. Almost every area had gale warnings – some described as severe – a state of affairs which, the broadcast promised, would extend to the North Sea.

That put paid to our trip to Norway, at least for the time being. Instead, we decided to head for Orkney; Wick, the nearest port, was no place to run for in an easterly gale.

Even more importantly, the Orkneys and Shetland were the only areas free from the threat of gales. At that stage we were sailing across the Pentland Firth with five rolls in the mainsail and no jib. Since we were being set down to leeward, and drawn towards the Pentland Firth, we started the engine to help keep us back on track. It was foul and wet. Huge sheets of spray broke over the bow and splattered over the cockpit. However, our navigation was OK – land showed up in the right place at the right time – and we finally made it into the shelter of Holm Sound.

The chart warned us that the channel was blocked – although a later correction said *partly* blocked. In either case, we hoped it would all be obvious as we approached – which indeed it was. The ships used to block the channel stood out clearly and, thanks to a fair wind, we sailed through them without any trouble and anchored in St Mary's

Bay. It felt good. By that time it was really blowing hard and pouring with rain; enough was enough.

Going down below, I was surprised to see how dry the boat was. With so much rain and spray, I was expecting the worst. The only bit that got really soaked was my clothes locker. I thought I'd been clever and picked the driest spot on the boat – but clearly, I got it wrong; it was by far the wettest!

By then, there were gale warnings for Orkney too, so we were glad to be snug and safe. Even so, as a precaution, we put out an extra anchor.

Next morning, we had what might best be described as a difference of opinion.

John was threatening to allow his sprouting stubble to develop into a proper, full-grown beard. After some wifely persuasion he retired below but returned with the job half done. Noticing his unbecoming side whiskers, I was less than restrained this time. After my rude remarks, he finally removed the lot.

With everything back to normal, we went ashore and dried our clothes at the local inn. There was no alcohol there because Orkney was dry – but we enjoyed sitting in the kitchen in front of a roaring fire watching our host's wife making bare bannocks, a cross between a bun and a pancake.

Later on, the couple gave us a lift to Kirkwall which has a fine cathedral with Norse connections. We spent the next few days exploring the Orkneys. At one place the locals told us they'd never seen a yacht before.

Our passage to the Shetlands was grim. A phlegmatic note in the log brought it all back. "John says ship's biscuits got wet but still taste nice."

As we closed in on Mousa Island, there was nothing to see, so we decided to carry on for another quarter of an hour. If nothing turned up we would head out to sea and heave-to. But suddenly we spotted the mail ship and, there, behind her, was land. What a relief. We carried on to Lerwick and moored up in the inner harbour.

Our arrival caused something of a sensation. People were running around to look at us and everyone wanted to help. As John explained to them, all he wanted was a hot bath and some food. In response, they pointed to a hotel on the other side of the harbour.

I could hardly wait. It was the most enjoyable bath – and most delicious eggs and bacon – that either of us could ever remember.

We also felt rather proud. Eighty-five miles in fifteen and a half hours meant an average of more than five knots – which was pretty good going for a boat which measured a mere twenty-three and a half feet on the waterline.

The following day, we dropped in on the coastguard who showed us the recent weather statistics which he logged for the Met Office. The previous day had seen winds of Force 8 with 'very high' seas. All of which, it seemed, put paid to Norway.

We were due home for a wedding on July 4th and time was running out. It was bitterly disappointing and although I appeared resigned, I was secretly determined to get across if the weather improved.

From Lerwick, we had a super sail to Hamna Voe, a delightful, landlocked harbour surrounded by tiny, isolated crofts. Even the hills looked barren and bare.

Once ashore, we were welcomed by a chap called Robbie Robertson. Mr Robertson had never seen a train, though he had seen a yacht – but only once before.

The weather forecast on June 9th spoke of an anticyclone and fair weather.

It was all too tempting. Messing about in the Shetlands might be fun but was a poor substitute for the famous Norwegian fjords. So, with eggs, milk and water supplied by Mrs Robertson we set forth. In bright sunshine and a light, southerly breeze, we sailed south-south-east for Norway.

After a couple of days, during which the weather stayed much the same, we spotted mountains – dim, blue Norwegian mountains, about forty miles off.

As the wind freshened, the motion became violent and we had to reef. It was cold, but the sun was still shining and our spirits were high.

As we approached, it was difficult to make out where we were because all the marks and beacons seemed exactly alike. So, we ran down the coast hoping to find an obvious landmark. After a while we reached a small island, which looked inviting, so we sailed round to leeward, near a fishing boat, and heaved to. The fishermen only spoke Norwegian but understood our predicament. When we shouted 'Marstennen' they pointed south.

Following their directions, after ten miles, we spotted a lighthouse and were soon safely tied up in Farne fjord. After a supper of scrambled eggs, hot coffee and rum, our tiredness disappeared and we felt absolutely fine.

We slept late and spent the next morning chatting to the locals, most of whom spoke excellent English. A party of holidaymakers invited us out for tea and the local boatbuilder took us back to his house. Everyone was so friendly here but, as we discovered as we visited other areas, that's not unusual. The Norwegians are an incredibly hospitable people, so after a while, we almost got used to it.

Next, it was on to Bergen through a winding passage among numerous islets and rocks.

It was fascinating. After picking up a mooring off the local yacht club, the Commodore came out to welcome us and insisted on our using the facilities as much as we liked.

We spent the next few days in Bergen where we booked a passage home on a steamer for the wedding in England. Then, we made the most of it. After all, this was the climax – and the reason why we came. So we indulged ourselves, with long, lazy hours motoring and sailing through narrow channels, and around clusters of fascinating islands which seemed to go on forever.

As we neared Eivindvik, the landscape changed. Lofty hills heaved into view.

There was green grass and trees, right up to the edge – with the sun, playing like a spotlight, on the deep blue, snow-capped mountains in the background – and making ever-changing shapes in the water.

Sailing up the magnificent Sogne fjord, the weather was perfect – so was everything else.

We were greedy for more; there were other fjords, branching off in different directions, so on we went – until the wind went fickle and it started to rain. Then, to cap it all, the engine started playing up. Engulfed by clouds of smoke, we quickly shut it down.

While John spent the next couple of hours trying to find out what was wrong, we drifted gently backwards for a quarter of a mile.

Eventually, all became clear: the engineers had fitted a drain tap to the exhaust by simply soldering it in place. The joint had melted, leaving a hole. Fortunately there was no immediate danger of fire or explosion – but in a more vulnerable position the consequences could have been extremely serious. John applied an asbestos bandage to the damaged area and we managed to make Balholm.

This particular port was popular with cruise liners – and the locals warned us that when a ship was in, everyone put up their prices. Forewarned was forearmed.

At Fjærland, we went on an excursion to look at some glaciers. Never having seen one before, I was both thrilled and impressed. While eating our lunch, we watched the nearby Suphelle glacier shedding huge chunks of ice which came crashing down, scattering fragments like powder. It was awesome.

It was here, in Fjærland, that we met the daughter of Hans Dahl, the celebrated Norwegian artist, who invited us home and showed us her father's studio. His paintings were exceptionally beautiful.

The weather was varied – with plenty of rain. When it stopped though, and the sun came out, everything was back to its beautiful best. I remember one evening in particular.

Tied up near a gigantic cliff, we watched no less than nine cascading waterfalls.

They plunged, unforgettably downward, into glassy water, tinged red from the reflection of a sun which was shining through the clouds.

Over the next few days we worked our way south then had our first minor mishap.

At Vikingvaag we anchored at six thirty in the evening and settled down to cook some fish which one of the locals had given us. We were moored head to wind between two rocks, with warps at bow and stern, and an anchor at right angles to take the strain should the wind shift onshore.

It was already blowing hard, with plenty of rain for good measure, but we went below to enjoy our freshly cooked supper. Before turning in around ten, we stuck our heads out to see if all was well. It wasn't. The wind had shifted to the south-west and was blowing straight onshore. Nevertheless, we weren't particularly worried. After all, we'd taken sensible precautions and were adequately prepared. Except for one thing. What we weren't prepared for was the soup-like characteristics of the bottom. In no time, we were dragging our anchor and heading for the rocks.

There were particular dangers here. Unlike the fjords of Sogne, Vikingvaag is comparatively shallow, with low-lying rocks around the edge, so we started the engine and brought the stern line forward. That quietened her down a bit but we were still far from happy so decided to release both the warps and motor over to the other side, which seemed fairly sheltered, and drop the anchor attached to forty-five fathoms of chain – which was as much as we had. Surely, we reasoned, that would be enough to stop her dragging?

As expected, the anchor came up all too easily, so we released the warps and eased the gear lever forward. Just then, the engine went mad and started revving furiously –

but the boat wasn't moving. Clearly, there was something round the prop so we quickly dropped the anchor again but, as before, it failed to get a grip – and we started drifting sideways towards the shore. With our mooring warps still attached to the rocks, the only rope I could find was a heaving line. I grabbed hold of it, bent it on to the kedge and passed it to John who, using every last ounce of energy, heaved it over the side, pitching it as far as he could.

Luckily, it held. We then took another small anchor and attached it to thirty fathoms of brand new, one and a half inch rope, along with our spare halyards, and took it out to windward. He then managed to get hold of one of the mooring warps which was still secured to the rock, and, by attaching it to some of our last remaining ropes, bring it back on board. That meant we had two anchors out, as well as a warp ashore. Even so, we were still lying broadside on.

After close examination, we discovered that the line securing the anchor buoy was still round the prop and holding her by the stern. In spite of that, we were lying fairly steady – and holding our position – so we went below and climbed, fully clothed, into our cosy, welcoming bunks. The shenanigans, which had lasted for two hours in a howling gale and pelting rain, had left us exhausted.

Next morning, things were little better. It was still wet, and the wind was still screaming, so we spent the day sorting everything out. Mr Vikingvaag brought a friend along and helped us free the prop and collect the warps – and we eventually restarted the engine which sounded a little lumpy. John thought the plugs were probably dirty and gave them a really thorough clean, after which it seemed a lot better.

In the evening, we went ashore for some milk but had to wait around for a couple of hours. Why? Well, young Miss Vikingvang had to trot off to milk the cows – and they lived in a field about six miles away. To be honest, it wasn't a problem because we spent the time chatting with her parents in their nice, warm kitchen.

Next morning, we made an early start. There was still a bit of misty rain about but the wind had dropped so our passage to Bergen was hardly record-breaking. We anchored off the yacht club at lunchtime, just as the sun came out.

The Club kindly agreed to look after *Mary Helen* in our absence and the following day, a Friday, we left aboard the SS *Vega* and got into Newcastle in time for John's brother's wedding. However, we were back in Bergen again on Sunday.

As you can see, we both found cruising in small boats totally addictive. That's why, all those years later, setting off across the Atlantic seemed a perfectly normal thing to do...

Chapter Four

FIRST NIGHT AT SEA

So there we were, Donald and I, having completed our first night at sea, after leaving Lagos, heading west in bright sunshine.

Later on that day we spotted three other yachts astern. Our trusty ship held two of them off but the third slowly overhauled us.

The sunset that evening was an unusually deep pink. It's funny how you appreciate such things at sea – and how significant they become. Just before midnight, the porpoises arrived, leaving torpedo-like tracks across our bows. They stayed with us for about ten minutes then left on more important business. The stars were out, the moon shone brightly and *Mary Helen* was striding along at 5¼ knots. This was fun.

The next day was slightly more cloudy but still basically sunny – and in spite of a north-westerly swell, the sea was slight and we had the ocean to ourselves.

Slowly, the north-north-westerly wind backed to the north-west and fell light which affected our speed.

Once again, the night was clear but the wind was even lighter. Even so, we resisted any temptation to start the engine until what wind there was headed us. However, at 1230 on Saturday, September 22nd 2000, we finally gave in and continued under power.

We saw several ships during the day; one came quite close. Donald said she was probably some sort of Liquid

Petroleum Gas (LPG) carrier with large round tanks where her holds should be.

During the afternoon clouds began building up and several showers passed through.

The wind also returned – about Force 3 this time, from the north, so, at 1715, the engine was relieved of its duties.

With more wind, the sea began building up and the odd slop or two found its way on board – but nothing would hold us back. Our little boat was eager and willing.

A sturdy north-easterly breeze, which held throughout the night and kept our spirits up, died slowly during the day, bringing our speed down to two to three knots. The sea was moderate with a pronounced swell from the north. Progress had been good and our ETA at Porto Santo was 1900 the following evening.

The next day was warm and sunny. The bow wave chuckled and we both felt happy and relaxed.

Approaching the appointed time for our landfall, the first thing we saw were lights – probably a fleet of fishing boats, we thought, but as we approached, they started rising – climbing higher and higher. Then slowly, everything fell into place. At 1942, three distinctive peaks were clearly visible on the horizon against the failing light.

By midnight, the loom of Ilheu de Cima also showed up.

The night was dark; there was no moon. Having been pushed along slowly, at about three knots, we arrived at dawn. A yacht which had been overhauling us fell back and was soon well astern. Quite right too.

It's at times like these that you realise just how useful radar is for giving you an accurate distance off. We never had anything like it in the good old days but it's definitely makes things easier. At night, in particular, it's easy to underestimate.

By daybreak, we had the complete picture. The marina answered our VHF call immediately and we were greeted by the harbour master who found us an excellent berth. The only drawback was all the tedious paperwork. Whatever happened to the EEC and free movement. It's horrendous!

After a proper rest, we set to work. There were several odd jobs to be done; this would be the last decent opportunity to sort everything out. One of our main concerns was the louvered companionway doors which, we thought, might ship too much water below should a heavy sea break over the stern. To be honest, I'd never worried about it before and the boat had never given us any cause for concern – not even during some seriously lumpy stuff on the way out – but, as always, better safe than sorry, so we waterproofed them with a pair of stout plywood covers.

While we were beavering away, we heard that Ian, my second son, who was circumnavigating the world in his 39-foot cruiser *Independent Freedom*, would be shortly leaving Gibraltar. The plan was to rendezvous at Lanzarote, our next port of call.

In the meantime, it was time to behave like tourists and do some sightseeing. Outside the town itself we found a general air of decay. Clearly, in the dim distant past, the island had once supported a thriving farming community but now, all that remained were crumbling agricultural terraces, abandoned cottages, and ash-like earth strewn with red and brown rocks. Exactly what went wrong, no one knows for sure, though according to one theory, it was all the fault of the rabbits. Apparently, our rapacious, furry friends destroyed the foliage that helps create clouds, which in turn produce rain.

Whatever the truth of it, at least the EEC has helped out with money to develop harbour facilities for yachts. The only problem with that, it seems, is a problem with staff.

Of course, it's difficult for outsiders like us to pass definitive comment about these things after such a brief stay – but what we saw with our own eyes was a sense of decline; everything needed freshening up. It's a pity because I imagine the business potential is enormous.

The island itself has numerous volcanic features with steep cliffs to the north and east, which contrasts with nine kilometres of beautiful sandy beaches to the south.

We also wandered into the town for the start of the famous Columbus Festival which gave us the opportunity to see the great explorer's house – or, at least, one of them; there were Columbus houses everywhere!

In the main square, we watched a colourful flag dance. The participants made a few mistakes but, in a way, that only added to the charm. They were so vivacious and enthusiastic.

The following day, a replica of the *Santa Maria* left the harbour to anchor off the town and put Christopher Columbus ashore. He was greeted by parades, pageants and pretty girls.

Naturally, perhaps, we wanted to sail to Funchal before heading south to the Canaries. However, after talking to the local R.C.C. representative, decided against it. From what he told us, it seemed the port was chaotic and overcrowded. Instead, therefore, we booked a day-trip by plane.

So it was then that on Tuesday October 3rd 2000 we rose early and climbed aboard a taxi which took us to the airport. When we reached Madeira, we hired a car and drove to Funchal; the old town is a warren of steep and winding roads.

The *QE2* was alongside, and dominated everything; the marina was scruffy and absolutely packed. Some skippers had managed to squeeze their boats in alongside the quay which looked far from peaceful; others were anchored outside and rolling awkwardly in a nasty swell. I didn't know which option was worse – but was grateful we'd given the place a miss.

Once through Funchal we headed west where, here and there, people were harvesting bananas.

Unlike the northern region, which produces grapes in abundance, in the south, the hill terracing seemed considerably more neglected.

The terrain is generally steep and precipitous although at four thousand five hundred feet, beyond the drizzle and rain, you find a plain. It's mostly scrub, but we noticed some recently planted firs. We were also impressed to see how steep the hillsides were; falling away in places into what were once volcanic craters.

From here, we descended to the north coast along narrow, meandering roads clinging to the hillsides. Eventually we arrived back at the airport having completed a complete circumnavigation.

The next day was spent preparing for the passage to Lanzarote.

Chapter Five

LUTINE GOLD

Before we could leave Porto Santo, we had to tell the police. What a waste of time; it was never like this in the old days – but, I suppose, things have changed and now, wherever you go in the world, form filling and security checks are simply something you have to live with.

One good thing came out of all this – we had time to get our weather fax working.

Such modern contraptions are a far cry from our humble old barograph but, had they been around then, I'm sure John would have bought one. To be honest though, while having the ability to print out up-to-date weather charts at the touch of a button undoubtedly makes sense, I still have mixed feelings about modern technology. Perhaps it's just nostalgia. Anyway, say what you will, even the cleverest piece of equipment can't guarantee good weather – and what the magic box told us in Porto Santo was far from comforting. The prediction was wind from the east and plenty of it. We would have to wait and see if the microchips had got it right.

As I say, it all seemed a lot less complicated before the war.

I suppose I was thinking about our first cruise in Norway again. Yes, I was younger then, so perhaps, that has something to do with it, but still, the abiding memory is one of ease and simplicity. I remember that summer in 1938, returning from the wedding in England and feeling a mixture of excitement and relief. I was fully aware of what was going on in the world – but had no idea that we were so close to war.

The strange antics of goose-stepping Germans seemed somehow irrelevant. We were back on the boat, our own boat, our small, floating home which could take us wherever we wanted – and in no time, we were off – wriggling through narrow channels and marvelling at the breathtaking scenery.

In those days, owning a boat was like belonging to a club, a small club, and people made you welcome wherever you went. Everything was more personal and more individualistic. You never felt like a tourist.

In Lunde, for example, we met a man with a very impressive name. Mr Lunde of Lunde. He was a boatbuilder who invited us back to his home for refreshments and showed John his drawings, models and pictures. They got on famously.

Then, in Rosendal, we went to see some of Mr Lunde's creations in the flesh.

Again, John was absolutely fascinated.

The sun was shining; the scenery was super. We even got a glimpse of the snow-covered mountain tops at the head of Hardanger Fjord where a retired ship's captain and lighthouse keeper came aboard and insisted on showing us the local seventeenth century castle. To reach it we had to walk through a green wooded valley. We felt a bit like characters in a Scandinavian fairy story. Indeed, the castle was the centre of many interesting tales but, at that time was being used as a holiday centre for Oslo professors.

We also visited the local church which was built of stone – but without a spire – highly unusual in Norway.

As I say, it was idyllic. But as every small boat skipper knows, nothing stays the same for long. Of course, had we owned a weather fax machine then, we might have been better prepared. We might even have missed mother nature's next surprise altogether.

On the other hand, in spite of the dangers, I'm glad we didn't...

We left in a strong but fickle breeze which really got the boat moving. I wrote in the log, 'Mary Helen skimmed over the water like a seaplane!'

However, approaching the Enaes light, the wind went wild, with terrific squalls and driving rain. The chop was amazing for such an apparently sheltered area; the entire surface of the water seemed to be peeling off in sheets and stopping us dead in our tracks – even with the engine screaming away at maximum revs. Although under bare poles, we were still almost laid flat; had we set any sail beating into it like that, we might have lost the mast.

It was hopeless. There was no way we could continue. The Sundal anchorage would have to wait; we would have to turn back. That meant hoisting the staysail. We turned, and started flying – at least, that's what it felt like – until another squall hit us from the opposite direction and the mast started flexing like a fishing rod. This was serious.

We dropped the sail and started the engine. Strong winds we could deal with, but such unpredictable gusts were simply too much.

I'm not given to exaggeration but these were heart stopping moments. If you don't believe me, try sailing up Mauranger Fjord in a gale and you'll see what I mean.

Either way, the local fishing boats certainly weren't taking any chances. Scurrying for shelter, they were hugging the south shore – from where most of the worst gusts were coming – so we decided to follow suit. Even then, we still shipped some water over the rails. Further on though, the sea gradually flattened out.

By the time we got back to Rosendal, the sun was shining again, so we spent time drying our clothes and easing our aching muscles.

It felt good and, earlier discomforts apart, we looked back on a day of sheer excitement.

I wouldn't have missed it for anything.

At dinner that evening, in the local inn, we enjoyed a simple but satisfying meal in the company of a charming Norwegian doctor and his sister. When we told them about our encounter with the darker side of Norwegian weather, they started talking about the church without a spire, the one we saw the day before. It was built that way, they explained, because of the fearsome winds. Now, it all made sense!

Next morning they dropped by and presented us with a lovely bunch of 'Roses from Rosendal'.

We left, with a little more temerity, on July 9th and once again, hit some powerful squalls but, this time, successfully completed the passage to Lervik, some twenty-two miles to the south.

When we got in, we met some people whose jib had blown out in the gusts. At least we arrived with all our sails intact.

We spent the evening singing, or trying to sing, traditional Norwegian songs aboard another nearby boat; a great way to unwind.

Then we set sail for Haugesund, dipping our ensign to the SS *Vega* which had taken us back to Newcastle. As she politely answered our salute, I wondered whether anyone on board remembered who we were.

During this stage of the cruise occasional showers gave way to incessant rain. Gone were the rolling hills and snow-capped mountains; here, everything was desolate and flat.

Having tied up, we went shopping in the drizzle, but later continued on to Koppervik, about eight miles away, and brought up alongside the quay.

To cap it all, the chops we'd bought for supper had gone bad, so John went up on deck and consigned them to the deep. Hearing a cry of astonishment, I poked my head out to see what was going on. To my amazement, I saw our Vice Commodore of the R.C.C., T. N. Dinwiddy, aboard his boat *Svenska* which was anchored in the southern inlet. It was so unexpected and such a pleasant surprise that we arranged to meet for dinner; we spent the evening swapping yarns. It was at that point that we opted to work our way south, then sail down the Danish and Dutch coasts instead of making a passage straight to England as originally intended.

More rain arrived on July 12th, so we shuttled back and forth to *Svenska* – before soaking up a little of the local colour. Some people cruise to exotic ports and spend time at casinos; John took me to Koppervik and showed me round a factory which processed sardines. I can still remember the smell.

Then off to Stavanger – not wearing oilskins for once! With so many rocks and islets about it looked tricky – and, we agreed, would be particularly testing in bad visibility. Fortunately conditions were ideal, so, with an excellent chart, it was all perfectly straightforward.

On arrival, we went ashore to pick up some money. Having only wired home a request the previous day, we were delighted to find it ready and waiting for us.

Who needs hole-in-the-wall cash dispensers!

Shortly afterwards we were joined by *Svenska*, and we all celebrated with a super salmon supper. Our Vice Commodore contributed generous supplies of strawberries and cream.

On Friday July 15th, we slipped quietly away from Stavanger in the early hours of the morning. It was pouring with rain and the visibility was rotten. We passed *Svenska* in the mist. Her skipper had heaved-to for breakfast, the sensible fellow. Later on, off Jederen Rev, she passed us under power. We were making slow progress in a light southerly, and gave her a wave.

I can't pretend that the scenery was anything but flat and boring. It was at about this point that a damp, exhausted pigeon decided to join us. We named it The Rev Jederen which seemed to meet with its approval because it stayed for a couple of days. We had the droppings to prove it!

The rain was penetrating but as soon as we approached Egersund, it stopped completely. Entering smooth water, we enjoyed a memorable trip up the narrow passage which leads to the town. Not surprisingly, *Svenska* was already in and waiting for us.

That evening we accompanied the Vice Commodore to a local inn and made the most of an excellent supper.

The next morning, while John was busy stowing all the provisions and filling up with water and fuel, I made some strawberry jam. Jolly good it was too!

While all this was going on, we noticed that *Svenska* had a visitor – an earnest looking young woman who, it seemed was trying to sell him something. We chuckled to ourselves – until the Vice Commodore pointed in our direction – and she made a beeline for us. She was some kind of missionary, it transpired, who promptly offered us a selection of religious tracts. When we told her we were heathens and entirely beyond redemption, she left us a leaflet entitled 'Jesu commelt shark'. In spite of that, no ill befell us, so I think we survived more or less unscathed.

In the afternoon, we slipped away from Egersund in company with *Svenska*. This was more like it; the sun shone as we gently beat our way along the coast. It was perfect weather for taking pictures – and *Svenska*'s skipper was soon clicking away. Whenever the wind dropped we motored for a bit but eventually there was nothing left, not even a breath, so we followed *Svenska* into Naalauvigen, the most perfect little harbour imaginable. In the bay, whilst taking down our sails, *Svenska* made a suddern turn towards the rocks and vanished. We chased after her – through a narrow entrance, with literally inches to spare – and found ourselves in a tiny landlocked basin not much bigger than a hockey pitch.

We anchored among some fishing boats but also decided to take some lines ashore to hold her steady. No sooner had we sorted everything out than our Vice Commodore joined us for supper. At the same time we heard a tap on the hull. It was a fisherman bearing fish. At first we thought he was trying to sell them but no, "it's a present!" he assured us. When we invited him on board he told us how local fishermen like him had dug the harbour themselves. Apparently, since the bay was open to the south-west, you invariably encountered a nasty swell outside. But here, all was calm. Their boats would be safe whatever the weather. It could blow a hurricane from any direction without ruffling their feathers.

As you might imagine, we listened intently and with great interest; this was precisely the kind of out-of-the-way place that appealed to people like us. It was perhaps fitting therefore that two R.C.C. yachts were anchored there at the same time.

Our next stop was Farsund which we finally reached after a somewhat wet and windy day. The sun tried hard to shine through but, on this occasion, its best just wasn't good enough. Still, the port was attractive and extremely well sheltered.

Next morning, I was woken by the sun which clearly, was trying to make amends for previous misdemeanours, so I scurried ashore and scrambled up the hills like a schoolgirl. I remember that feeling even now. It just felt good to be alive.

In the afternoon we set off in a fresh north-westerly wind bound for Lim fjord in Denmark. It was perfectly OK sailing in the lee of the islands – in fact it was more than OK – and we charged along enjoying the view. But once out in the open we felt the full force of the weather and ran into pretty rough water.

After crashing about for a bit, *Svenska*'s skipper made the seamanlike decision to call it off and got close enough to indicate his intentions. He suggested we make for a bolt-hole round the Lindesnes, so we fell in astern, and after a hairy gybe round the headland were back in sheltered waters. By evening, after threading our way through a maze

Onaway, sailing north, 1925.

Emanuel, aground in the Parret, 1929.

▲ Skipper at the helm.

▼ Emanuel.

The Faeroes, 1929. Drying fish at Trangisvaag.

The skipper and mate (on the right) with the Petersens.

Traditional Faeroese boat at Thorshavn Typically 21 ft loa, with a 6 ft beam, they have the shape of old Viking ships. Most were fitted with engines, but we saw several sailing with a small sprit-rigged mainsail.

Thorshavn's postmaster looking smart in national dress.

▲ The Padstow lifeboat, *Princess Mary*, 1930.

Alain Gerbault, the intrepid transatlantic yachtsman, signing my programme at the RCC Jubilee party in 1930.

▼

Luxury living. Caravans have undoubtedly improved, but Mum loved her mobile home. Here we are eating *al fresco* at Loch Duich in 1933. I can't remember what the spade was for…

◀ Scrubbing off at Helford. She sailed much faster after this.

Wedding day, Bridgewater 1936. John, me and *Emanuel*.
▼

◀ John, Dad and me sailing *Emanuel* in the 1935 Round the Island race.

▲ *Mary Helen* drifting along.

▲ Heading North in 1938. *Mary Helen*, safe and sound in Lerwick, Shetland.

▲ At Vik in Norway.

▶ Norwegian fisherboy at Koppervik with lobsters.

▲ Dozens of children came out to see the strange craft in their harbour – and they clearly enjoyed the sweets we gave them.

▲ En route for Denmark.

▲ Me at the helm.

◀ A traditional fishing boat on the Zuider Zee.

Hitching a ride to Haarlem – our friendly Dutch cyclist.

▼

◀ At Volendam on the Zuider Zee.

My John, *Mary Helen's* designer. I think he would have been proud of us.

Seadogs – John with Donald and Ian. Note the slim-line lifejackets.

of captivating islets under a warm and benevolent sun, we were anchored in a charming bay behind Svenevig island in Remes Fjord. It was still blowing hard the following morning so we went for a picnic. The locals gave us some strawberries which were so good, we bought some more for supper.

Finally, on Thursday, July 21st we were Denmark-bound again. The breeze was moderate and we chortled along at an acceptable four knots. By the afternoon though, it tailed off and we had to start the engine. On that basis, by our reckoning, we could expect to pick up land in the early hours of Friday morning.

But when the time came, instead, all we saw was fog. So, in order to get a rough idea of our position, and as a safety check, we took a sounding with the lead and measured fifteen fathoms. Half an hour later we were down to eleven fathoms, which still gave us more than enough water, but the next one recorded seven fathoms. Not only that, we could now hear the crunching, spluttering sound of breakers. The situation was made all the more worrying because the Lodbjerg lighthouse should have been relatively close, but since it didn't have a fog signal, and because we couldn't see it, it was impossible to know exactly where we were. So, at 0500, rather than attempting a strange entrance in minimal visibility, we decided to drop the anchor. Because we still had our sails set, we lay very quietly. Actually, as *Mary Helen* rose gently in the swell, it felt rather pleasant – like being in some snug, sheltered anchorage. Of course, nothing could be further from the truth, and we knew it, so we kept a proper watch. By 0700, the fog lifted. I could now not only hear the breaking waves; I could see them too. Soon, I managed to make out the shore – and then, about a mile to the north, and exactly as predicted, the Lodbjerg lighthouse emerged; most reassuring. We got underway almost immediately and proceeded into Thyborøn

By that time, the entrance was perfectly clear – though, in the channel itself, the swell was quite pronounced. Once safely inside we came alongside our old friend *Svenska* who had beaten us to it!

With the fog gone and the sun streaming down it was almost too hot to go shopping – but duty called and off I went. When I returned, I stupidly managed to drop a jar of honey which smashed to pieces on the quay. As a finale, while trying to pick up the pieces, I somehow managed to lose the rest of our stores which fell neatly into the harbour.

The water looked so dark and filthy that any attempt at salvage would have been utterly pointless so I gave up and went back to the boat. By that time our stomachs were rumbling but since there was nowhere to eat or drink, we all decided to make for Lemvig in the afternoon. That evening we tucked into an excellent meal ashore with the Vice Commodore. Food tastes so much better when you're starving.

Next day, after lunch, we said goodbye to *Svenska* who was going home via the Kiel Canal. Our route would take us along the coast, via Holland, so we returned to Thyborøn. The north-west wind was extremely light which meant we had to motor most of the way. The engine itself was a bit cranky but it just about managed. Once there, I boiled a chicken we'd bought in Lemvig. It cost 'one and six' – or about seven and a half pence in today's money – and tasted absolutely brilliant.

When it was time to leave, while hoisting the sails, we somehow managed to knock the anchor winch handle overboard. It was an essential piece of equipment – and as we imagined trying to weigh the anchor by hand, in some deep and dangerous bay, in bad weather perhaps, or in the middle of the night, we realised we couldn't leave without one.

The following day was a Sunday – but when John went ashore for some milk, he found a blacksmith working in his smithy. What a stroke of luck! Somehow, John made himself understood and persuaded the chap to come aboard. Neither spoke the other's language, so trying to explain what we wanted involved a combination of gesticulations, sign language and grunts. In the end though, our man seemed to understand and John took him ashore. An hour later, we had a truly marvellous new winch handle which cost us three Kroner. John was delighted and extremely grateful.

By 1115 we were off. During the morning, we passed close to the Horns Rev Lightship and they dipped their ensign to us. Of course we answered. It was quite a moment as they all waved; such a friendly gesture. We had quite a frustrating morning though. We hoisted the yankee, then lowered it again. It rained and, as usual, the engine played up. My old log painted a gloomy picture, 'sick engine, sick wind, pretty foul'.

Then the engine died altogether, so we drifted. Finally, we got a puff of wind and started to move again – but painfully slowly; we were crawling along at about 1 or 2 knots!

On Wednesday, July 27th we sighted the Ameland lighthouse – and took a sounding but failed to find the bottom even at 9 fathoms; the log read 213 nautical miles.

We managed to get the engine going again, but it still sounded dodgy. In the evening we decided to try for Ameland Zeegat.

The following morning we had a lie-in because the tide we needed to catch to help us on our way to Terschelling wasn't until late morning. There was a moderate easterly breeze so our hopes were high – but alas, by 1030 the wind freshened from the west – right on the nose. Neither of us fancied a long slog to windward not to mention the anxiety of negotiating the notorious bars at the mouths of Ameland and Terschelling so we decided to stay put. To cap it all, we had the discomfort of a nasty short chop to deal with, so let out our full 40 fathoms of chain, and put a spring on the cable to reduce any snubbing. She lay very well though her motion at times was rather violent – and when the tide turned she was beam on, and got splattered by dollops of spray. The seas, though short, were also steep, with nasty breaking crests; an unhealthy combination. Nevertheless, we counted our blessings. It could have been worse. At least we'd spent a comfortable night – and after all, we could have been hove-to in the North Sea in a gale.

John spent most of the day tinkering with our troublesome engine while I did some Norwegian embroidery I'd bought in Bergen. I must have made a good job of it because I still have it with me today. Every time I look at it I'm reminded of that wet, windy and altogether desolate day in Ameland Zeegat.

Finally, John managed to put his finger on the problem; apparently the magneto was playing up. The bad news was that fixing it would be impossible without proper equipment so there was nothing for it: we had to soldier on. It was far from ideal of course because our troublesome two-stroke was only firing on one cylinder – but even that, we decided, was better than nothing.

The weather eased over night so, at 0400, and fortified by mugs of steaming hot cocoa, because it was far too early for breakfast, we got underway.

The wind was light and southerly – and the sunrise magnificent – though ominously red.

In the full glow of the early morning light, we purred along happily.

Gradually though, the wind freshened from the south-west, and by the time we reached the entrance to Terschelling Nord Gat, we were struggling. The big, grown-up breeze was flexing its muscles and having fun with the tide. It was blowing into its face and making it angry. Perhaps, given that boisterous and belligerent chop, we should have reefed, but we were anxious to get further up the channel and needed every ounce of power. We even started the engine, which, in spite of its obvious illness, added a little extra punch, as we see-sawed against the current.

After rounding up to Terschelling, everything changed. With a fair wind we bowled along in fine style and by lunchtime were safely tied up in the inner harbour. The town was buzzing and draped with flags. As far as we could make out, gold had just been recovered from the wreck of the *Lutine* which sank in October 1799. As you probably know, the ship's bell was subsequently recovered and taken to Lloyds of London where the underwriters ring it whenever there's an important claim. Anyhow, while *Lutine* herself has long been associated with ill fortune, we, it seemed, had brought the locals luck. At least, that's what they told us!

The next day we stayed put because the wind was so strong – but John went ashore to see about the magneto. Unfortunately, the town had gone completely mad and everyone was talking about the gold. So, since nobody seemed particularly interested in our problem we went Dutch and hired a couple of bicycles. Off we pedalled in search of a quiet beach, and were happily riding along in the middle of the road when a car approached.

It was really frightening because, for a moment, we couldn't remember which side of the road we should be on – and simply dismounted. We stood there, motionless and roaring with laughter. It was partly because we felt so stupid – and partly from a sense of relief as we watched the driver motor safely away. He must have thought we were mad.

On our return, we saw a newly arrived motorboat from England so hurried over to say hello. Unfortunately they thought we were Dutch and complimented us on our English!

On the Sunday it was really hot – in fact it was boiling – and we were still having trouble. Making face to face contact with anyone who could mend the magneto was proving difficult so we decided to have it sent to Amsterdam and sail without it.

That evening we received an invitation to a dance at the Badspavillon which we gratefully accepted. We needed some light relief and this was great fun; just what the doctor ordered. I ended up dancing with someone whose name, or, at least whose business, sounded strangely familiar. Then the penny dropped and I remembered reading advertisements in the nautical almanac run by someone based in Terschelling calling himself 'The Helping Hand of the North Sea'. My partner, it transpired, was the Helping Hand himself.

Next day, on August 1st we made the most of a steady, fair wind and made our way to the first lock constructed in the new barrier of the Zuider Zee. It was enormously exciting and we felt both privileged and elated to be exploring such an interesting area. The lock keepers were most friendly and helped organise our lines and fenders; they even made a telephone call to Amsterdam to try and track down a telegram we were expecting. After locating it, they kindly relayed the message to us. It was good news; there was no need to hurry home after all. It also meant we could stop worrying about the mechanical problems which had made us so late.

In a more relaxed mood, I decided to take advantage of the blistering heat. Stripping off, I tied myself to a line attached to *Mary Helen*'s stern and plunged over the side.

It was bliss. With the boat doing all the work, it was also effortless; I was towed gently through the water – and would have stayed there, had the wind not suddenly freshened. John was visibly relieved when I clambered back on board because he'd been terrified that someone might have seen me naked in the water!

Drying myself with a towel I noticed myriads of small yellowish-green flies with long tails. I don't know what they were but they certainly annoyed me – though, fortunately they didn't bite. Later on we were told that their presence was somehow a direct result of the dam, which had turned the water from salt to fresh. It was hard to follow, but whatever the cause, the problem had apparently been far worse earlier on – so, I suppose, that was something to be grateful for.

The next stop was Enkhuizen where we found an excellent berth on the south side of this fine, roomy harbour. We really enjoyed it here – and were most taken by the old picturesque Zuider Zee fishing boats beating in under sail.

However, for their owners, of course, things were dire. Draining the sea was having a devastating effect on the fish.

All they caught now were eels and minnows which they shoved unceremoniously on to lorries and sold for fishmeal and manure.

We set sail the following day in a fresh north-westerly breeze. Just outside the harbour I put the helm up and heard a crack. The tiller had snapped at the rudder head.

With *Mary Helen* charging full pelt towards the dyke, John quickly released the sheets while I leapt below. Finding the spare tiller, I thrust it up through the companionway where John immediately slotted it into place and got her going in the right direction. Panic over! We were particularly annoyed about the tiller because, convinced that the original one was too light, John had insisted on having it specially made just before we left Poole. Thank goodness we carried the first one as a spare.

Anyway, breathing a sigh of relief, we soon settled down for a cracking sail as *Mary Helen* bowled and rolled her away through the short, sharp Zuider Zee chop.

Approaching Amsterdam and the locks, we were sailing too fast, so had to reef, before finally lowering the sails altogether. Then on to Marken and up to the Sixhaven yacht harbour. It was perfectly straightforward, even without a detailed chart.

You simply sailed straight on until you saw the big buildings of the Central Station; Sixhaven was opposite with a flag flying at the entrance.

It was first rate – with excellent facilities so we were happy to stop over for a few days until the magneto arrived. During our stay there the famous yacht builder Vries Lentsch made us a lovely new laminated tiller; a real work of art. I don't remember any money changing hands but John got on well with the people in the yard so perhaps it was a present. The sad thing is it remained in use until about ten years ago, when during a refit, it mysteriously vanished.

We also visited the Rijksmuseum and admired the famous paintings there – along with their fine collection of model ships. We took a trip or what the locals call a 'round Vaart' in a motorboat, exploring the town's canals then hopped on a train and went to Volendam.

The place was over-run with visitors – to such an extent that, as our guide explained, few locals went fishing in the sea any more because fishing for tourists was eminently more profitable. Once again, here we were behaving like tourists ourselves, but because we'd sailed to Holland in our own boat, it seemed completely different.

The weather was wonderfully hot but just to be awkward I developed a cold.

We then worked our way through the canals. There were charges at some bridges, but not others; some opened on time, some didn't. At one, we met a young Dutch sailor who wanted to go to Haarlem so we gave him – and his bicycle – a lift.

At one stage, we arrived at an unmarked bridge in the middle of the day. We blew our hooter but nothing happened. Some of the passers-by smiled at us and put their palms together by the side of their face to signify sleep – which caused us concern. Could this be the dreaded bridge that only opened between 0600 and 0700? We'd been warned about it in Amsterdam but failed to find out exactly where it was. Since we'd only recently bought some expensive new charts, we assumed it would be marked. We'd even asked about it at the local Watertourism office but their response was somewhat vague – although we found out it was new, just north of the Kaag Lakes, and carried the main road from Amsterdam to The Hague.

Well, now we knew for sure. This was obviously it and there was nothing we could do. We tried though. We asked a helpful local to have a word with the people in charge, which he did – but, it seemed, rules were rules and the bridge remained obstinately shut.

Finally, we went ashore for tea in the Kaag Lakes Yacht Haven and cursed ourselves for being so casual. We weren't the only ones to get it wrong that day though; several other boats were forced to wait as well.

Suffice it to say we were up bright and early the following morning and, at 0600 the bridge duly opened to let three ships through from the south. But then, just as we were slipping our warps, it shut again. Calamity! Naturally, there was much anger and consternation on our side, and everyone started sounding their fog horns and hooters. Much to our relief however, it opened again, and all the boats got through.

Later, passing through a village along the canal, we noticed a milkman, so went alongside the quay to stock up. Stepping ashore, we saw a house with a sign in English. 'Dairy Farm Butter, Milk, Cheese and Eggs for the water sportsman,' it read.

It was just what we wanted so we knocked on the door, went in, stocked up with food, and even had breakfast there.

The sun was shining as we left. Once underway, the scenery drifted past like a tableau. Houses, gardens, cafes, fields, cows and, of course, ubiquitous windmills, appeared and reappeared, along with a towering, tall-spired church every hour or so for good measure.

We saved the drama for the bridges. At one of them, the swirling wash from a barge sent us charging into the ironwork. No harm was done but the bridge keeper lost his 'klompen' – a small Dutch clog which they use to collect the toll charge. They attach it to a line and lower it down, but on this occasion, I'd just put my coins in, and taken the receipt, when the boat lurched and it tangled in the rigging. I had my receipt but the klompen fell into the water taking the money with it.

We spent several more days in the canals, negotiating numerous bridges.

As before, some opened promptly and some didn't. One even charged 85 cents instead of the usual 20.

On August 10th, we slipped through the Juliana sluice and entered the tidal waters of the River Ijssel. Naturally, with our luck, the stream was against us but in the evening, we eventually tied up at Dordrecht. No sooner had we arrived than a man appeared from the shadows; a tiny fellow but forceful. He wanted to sell us provisions – but we were far too tired and hungry to think about such things, so asked him to recommend a convenient place to eat instead. He directed us to the Hotel Pension where we ordered supper.

It was actually pretty good and very reasonably priced. As we ate, we looked back on our trip through the canals. The thing that struck us most was the amazing amount of traffic – not to mention the international diversity. We even saw a Swiss ensign!

Our next stop was Willemstad where we lay in the inner harbour alongside a cargo boat. There was plenty of water here but outside, even at high water, there was no more than 9 feet.

After that, we set off for Flushing. Beating across the narrow and heavily congested Volkerak Channel we decided to start the engine – but this time it flatly refused to start. There was no alternative: we had to zig-zag our way through streams of heavy duty tugs towing gigantic barges. How they must have hated us.

At one point, while going forward to clear the headsheets, I lost one of my smart Norwegian shoes which fell in the water but miraculously stayed afloat. In spite of the difficult conditions we managed a successful 'shoe overboard' procedure and fished it out before it sank.

Our next encounter was with a fellow R.C.C. friend, George Naish sailing *Polestar* in the opposite direction. With a fair wind, he passed us, looking peaceful and relaxed; we envied him. To improve our lot, John opted for one final tussle with the engine which, quite unaccountably, started at once. I don't know what it is about Stuart Turners; when they decide everything's OK, they run like sewing machines, but, if, for any reason, they get moody or difficult, there's little you can do about it. Anyhow, that's the way it was with ours.

We locked into Veere, a fascinating little place but hot and windless – then tied up for a break in Middleburg. It was here that John decided to have a shave so we started the engine, which, for some reason, was still behaving itself, and filled a saucepan with piping hot water from the cooling system. It was quicker than lighting the Primus, and you could have as much as you liked. Suitably scrubbed and spruced, we went ashore and had a meal.

Finally, we made our way to Flushing where I wanted to meet up with the harbour master because I'd made friends with him in 1936 while sailing with Tim Morris in *Veryan*.

For that reason, we made fast to the stagings near the lock gates – even though the local yacht club wanted us to tie up just outside the basin. I was greeted like a long lost cousin, so it's just as well we did. The next day was spent at Flushing where we found someone to mend the glass in our skylight which for some inexplicable reason had cracked.

We locked out in the early hours of August 14th and had a pleasant sail to Ostende where we tied up alongside a convenient barge. After giving the owner's children some sweets, we turned in for a snooze. Awakened and refreshed we took a tram to Blankenberge and finished the day with a slap-up dinner in Ostende.

Next day we reached Dunkerque before the tide turned and anchored in five fathoms behind the floating dock.

As a diversion, we visited Malo les Bains and had enormous fun watching the French on holiday – and enjoying a tasty cheap meal at the Hotel Casino. We tried hard to leave Dunkerque, but on two occasions, having weighed both anchors and poked our nose outside, were turned back by the weather. So, we were stuck there.

To make the most of our time we caught a train to Ypres. It was sobering. British soldiers who fell there usually called it Vipers – but however you pronounce it, even today, the name is synonymous with carnage and waste.

Little did we know that little more than twelve months later, another generation of young men would be called upon to fight and, in many cases, die for their country.

And all that after the so-called War to End Wars. In 1918 my parents' generation thought that conflict on that kind of scale would never happen again. How wrong can you be?

With Ypres still casting a shadow, we finally got away on Sunday, August 21st, just after breakfast. By lunchtime England was in sight; it was thrilling.

Half the fun of going foreign is coming home again!

We got into Dover and anchored in the South-east basin at 1910. Next day, it was blowing a bit from the west, so since John was feeling under the weather, we stayed put. The thought of a long boring beat to the Solent was the last thing we wanted.

Next morning, everything had changed. The breeze was from the east and tempting us to leave. John was still feeling seedy but this was too good to miss. We were away by 0700, and enjoyed a fine morning's sailing. It was sunny, we had a fair wind and *Mary Helen*, under full sail, including topsail and yankee was having as much fun as we were. Eventually though, we were left with light airs, so we started the engine to catch the tide at Dungeness. Later with the wind right aft, we boomed the yankee out as a spinnaker. We must have looked pretty good as we passed the Royal Sovereign Light Vessel.

Having passed Beachy Head Light at about 2000, I had my spell below which lasted until midnight.

Twelve hours later we sailed into Portsmouth and beat into the yacht basin by Camper & Nicholson before homing in on a convenient mooring and making a tack with the idea of picking it up. We never made it. Instead we hit a mud bank on a falling tide.

It was pure carelessness. The obstacle was clearly marked on the chart so there was no one to blame but ourselves. What a comedown after sailing so far! Here we were, high and dry in Portsmouth Harbour for all the world to see. It would be midnight before we floated free. Rather than wait around, we managed to get ashore and had supper with friends. We got off OK on the following tide and lay alongside a coal barge for the rest of the night.

Off we went the following morning in a light northerly wind bound for Lymington, arriving at 1630 on August 26th.

That was the end of a marvellous summer, and a super cruise. We visited five countries and met dozens of interesting people. Who said travelling is the art of disappointment? John said we'd never have got so far without the engine; I begged to differ, though conceded that it might have taken longer.

Track of *Mary Helen* 1938

Chapter Six

ROUGH PASSAGE

Back in 1938 then, we successfully completed what for us was our maiden cruise, little knowing that the world was about to change. Now, at the end of the Millennium, here I was again, embarking on another voyage, in the same little boat. We weren't on the brink of war, this time, but without wishing to overdramatise, the events of 9/11 were, for different reasons, equally dramatic and, for the man in the street, equally unforseen.

As far as I'm concerned though, it reinforces my fundamental belief that you should make the most of your life – because nothing's certain except uncertainty.

Don't listen to the pessimists. Whatever you want to do, someone will tell you you can't. It's too difficult or too dangerous; you're either too young or too old. In fact, the time is never right unless you make it so. My advice therefore is simple: just get on and do it.

In that sort of mood, I watched the sky to see if our fancy weather fax had got it right. It was all too accurate. The wind was blowing from the east, and a good Force 3 or 4 and, at 0900 on October 5th 2000 we sprung *Mary Helen* through the wind and left Porto Santo astern, bound for Lanzarote.

Once outside, and clear of the land, we hardened the sheets and forged ahead at 5 knots. The sea was awkward and seemed determined to get on board. From time to time, *Mary Helen*'s bowsprit would stutter and drop as she scooped up a big one over the bows and dumped it back on deck. But the sun was shining, it wasn't cold, and we were making excellent progress. What did it matter if we got a little wet?

By nightfall the wind had increased and was heading us a touch. With the rail awash and the motion increasingly violent, it was time to reef.

There was something else, *Mary Helen* was beginning to make a little water. At first it was just a bucket a day; now it was two buckets every eight hours. Some of it was simply water from the cockpit draining into the bilges. Modern boats have watertight cockpits which are fitted with pipes and drains so that any water that finds its way on board automatically finds its way out again. Back in 1935 however such innovations were rare – and some people actually preferred conventional cockpits because, they said, it took too long for the water to drain out by itself – and, in the process, the extra weight at the stern would drag the boat down and make it vulnerable to seas breaking over the stern.

Whatever the respective merits, *Mary Helen* was very much a boat of the old school, and none the worse for that. The real problem was the volume of water coming in right now, which suggested a slight leak. It's not that unusual on an old wooden boat but it would be foolish to ignore it. That's why we took it easier; pounding into heavy seas for hour after hour is bound to take its toll. It reminded me of a similar situation many years before when, in 1969, having gained his Master's ticket, my second son Ian decided to come sailing with me in *Mary Helen* before going back to sea – which suited me fine. After working with big ships it must have been strange for him in a way because, of course, our little boat still relied on only the most basic aids to navigation. But perhaps that's what appealed to him! Anyhow, we set off on May 16th from Lymington, but about

12 miles out from the Needles, in a moderate south-westerly wind, she started leaking! Reluctantly, we decided to turn back in case it got worse. Having returned to the boatyard, half an hour later we were being ignominiously hauled out of the water by Berthon's new boat lift.

After a busy few days re-caulking her, we were off again on May 22nd; this time with John who stayed with us until we reached Cherbourg. I imagine he thought that if the caulking was unsatisfactory he might as well go down with her! However, all was well and we successfully crossed the Channel after a fairly hectic sail in a fresh easterly wind. The reason we aimed for Cherbourg, apart from the fact that we like the place and have several friends there, was to collect my duffle coat from the Café de Paris, which I left there the previous February. It was safely waiting for me and I must say I was jolly glad to have it because the weather was hardly tropical.

We saw John off on the Thoressen ferry. His parting shot was, "take care of her", meaning the boat of course, not me! It was such a horrid afternoon that we decided to stay put, but next day, Sunday, May 25th we sailed over to Alderney in a light breeze. There was such a crowd in the main harbour that we decided to anchor in the bay off the old pier – but went a bit too close, and grazed a rock as we passed. Having caught some mackerel on the way we enjoyed a tasty lunch but unfortunately it turned wet and windy in the afternoon so, as a precaution, we laid out the kedge.

The following morning was bright and sunny. With two rolls in the mainsail and working jib, and a fresh south-westerly wind, it was quite exciting entering the Alderney Race and negotiating frightening patches of overfalls, but *Mary Helen* performed brilliantly and thanks to the strong tide was soon safely through.

Later on we shook out the reefs and hoisted the genoa. Immediately, the wind piped up and it started to rain!

Alas, the wind soon disappeared and we had to start the engine; it was no fun lolloping about in a calm with the tide about to turn. The engine ran cheerfully for about ten minutes, then coughed and finally stopped, so we hoisted the big genoa. Even so, we still made only extremely slow progress against the tide. By 1500 Ian managed to get the engine going again and fifteen minutes later we were safely anchored in St Peter Port. Several R.C.C. friends were there, so we enjoyed a most sociable evening.

Next morning was spent shopping and sorting out the laundry. I also tried to get my spectacles mended though I can't remember how they got broken.

In the afternoon we thought it would be fun to run over to Havre Gosselin, so, since there was no wind, we motored across. In spite of the calm weather we encountered a huge swell and noticed how badly an anchored yacht was rolling, so we went back to St Peter Port.

On the May 28th we sailed out under full main and working jib, which we was smartly replaced by the genoa when we hit a lumpy sea off St Martin's. In rain and light breezes it took us from 0700 to 1630 to reach the entrance of Lézardrieux close hauled. However the sail up this delightful river, illuminated by a dazzling rainbow, was most enjoyable. We picked up a buoy off the quay in time for a super dinner ashore then returned to the boat and slept like logs.

Perros Guirec was our next port of call. We had a pleasant sail there in variable light winds, which petered out at the entrance of the harbour. The engine characteristically failed to start but we managed to drift in and tie up at the eastern breakwater, rather further out than usual. The harbour looked strangely different and when the tide went down we saw why! They were building a 'basin à flot' and there was a barricade all the way across from the fisherman's slip on the west side to the northern end of the eastern breakwater. They told us there would be a lock gate and that work was scheduled for completion in June. It was just as well that we hadn't ventured further in – and got stuck on the half finished barrier. Actually it was fun watching tractors buzzing about at the bottom of the harbour! Perros Guirec itself is just over the hill; it's a lovely little seaside town with a sandy beach.

We then sailed on to Morlaix in a fresh northerly wind. Having never been further west than Perros before, it was all new to us from then on. We particularly enjoyed the thrill of sailing up the lovely Morlaix river through beautiful wooded countryside, in the warm, relaxing sunshine. We got through the locks in the afternoon and tied up to a nearby pontoon. The imposing viaduct dominated everything.

Dr Pilet, an old R.C.C. friend dropped by to welcome us. What a difference a friendly face makes. When you arrive at a new port nowadays the first person you see is someone either asking for money – or telling you to move! Dr Pilet was also well up on local knowledge and recommended the Auberge des Gourments for dinner. It was excellent.

We were off early on June 1st and locked out at 0730. Unfortunately we just missed the tide which would carry us through the inner Roscoff channel, and spent a rather tedious day beating against a light westerly wind. It was midnight by the time we anchored off le Touris in l'Abervrac'h; the rocky entrance looked menacing but magnificent in the moonlight.

The following day brought light winds again, but there was lots of sun so we struggled on, sometimes under power, sometimes under sail.

We were unable to make St Mathieu on the tide so anchored in Anse de Blanc Sablons. The vivid, clean water and bright sunshine made me think of swimming – but I resisted the temptation! Ian went ashore to get some petrol and had to walk across the isthmus to Le Conquet. It was a long way in the heat. Later a breeze got up and we had a marvellous sail close inshore, finally finishing up anchored in Camaret off the lifeboat slip. Pte de Toulinguet and its rocks make a magnificent approach to Brest, and Camaret has an imposing entrance between high rocky cliffs.

It still seemed to be essentially a fishing port and we were intrigued to see the fishing boats hauled out sideways on the slip.

We sailed over to Brest in a fresh north-westerly wind and lay alongside a swishy motorboat, charmingly named *Vaya Con Dios*. Once ashore, I managed to get my spectacles mended, which was one up for Brest. However, since you can get duty free at l'Abervrac'h now, the only reason for going to Brest would be to get something repaired. On the other hand, once you've struggled up the hill there's a fine view, and I must say I did rather enjoy looking at some of the shops; some of them were very smart indeed.

After collecting my glasses and giving an Irish skipper a cup of tea – the poor chap had almost blown his boat up while messing about with the engine – we set off again for Camaret. Under headsail alone, in bright sunshine and a strong wind, *Mary Helen*, flanked by golden gorse gleaming on the clifftops, was almost surfing. Supper on board consisted of coq-au-vin and strawberries and cream!

We were off again early next morning beating out of Camaret under main and genoa. Sailing through the Toulinguet Channel, *Mary Helen* accelerated like a speed boat in the gusts. By midday we were through the Raz de Sein, but then the wind died away and we were left floundering. We started the engine which, uncharacteristically, started first go, and made for the thriving port of Guilvinec.

As we approached the entrance we met a solid phalanx of gaily coloured fishing boats spread right across the harbour. We made our way up to the quay by the fish market which, we were told, would be uncomfortable because of the constant comings and goings. (In fact, I think we were really in the way!). Anyway we found a berth a bit higher up where we moored to a barge alongside a new section of quay. Later, a small Dutch boat came in; we were the only yachts there.

We liked Guilvinec with its air of prosperity and genuine friendliness. Next day we woke to find the harbour empty!

We were soon gone too, and had several days of lovely quiet sailing in bright sunshine. It was really warm at last! On June 9th we entered the Morbihan. This was quite an exciting moment. We'd heard so much about the place, its tides, shoals and fluky winds etc – and it didn't disappoint.

We were totally enchanted with this large expanse of shimmering water, studded with fascinating woodland, myriad channels and numerous rocky islands. It was quite different from any preconceived ideas I may have had; I think I'd always pictured it as a vast area of mud and sand.

We realised of course, that there would indeed be plenty of mud at low water but the rest was a welcome surprise. We sailed up the Auray River in a gentle breeze, breathing the scents of pine, hay and gorse, and enjoying the peace and quiet. The next thing we saw was a spectacular splash of purple rhododendrons through the narrows at le Rocher; quite dazzling! There were poles of white concrete by most of the landing places, which intrigued us. Later on we discovered they were for oysters which would eventually be shipped off to the Coureau d'Oléron.

As we neared the top of the river the wind got fickle and fluky, but luckily the engine refused to start, so we had to keep sailing in spite of the fact that the burgee and ensign were blowing in opposite directions at one point. I was kept extremely busy handling the sheets. However, a puff at precisely the right moment brought us to the pool where we anchored just in time for lunch. In the afternoon we had a walk up to the ancient little town where we found lots of good shops and cafés, as well as a bank.

We saw *Serenity of Totnes* anchored below us, and I was happy to learn that my beloved *Emanuel* was still afloat and being well cared for.

There was no wind at all the following morning so, after trying for an hour trying to get the engine to go, Ian went ashore to find a mechanic. After another hour or so they eventually managed to start it again, and we set off for Vannes. It was fascinating weaving our way the through tortuous channels amongst the islands but at least the tide was in the right direction. Finally, we slipped up the tree-lined canal of Vannes with scabious, sea pinks, wild roses and honeysuckle on the banks and birds singing in the meadows. We tied up to a convenient quay and went ashore for stores and a drink at the quayside café.

The town looked interesting and I wished I knew more about architecture, but anyway we couldn't spend long there because it dries at low water and we needed to catch the tide to take us back. Finally we picked up a mooring off Ile de Conleau, where, after a pleasant walk ashore, we had a good dinner at the hotel which was less expensive than it looked.

Next morning, after Ian had had his usual struggle with our reluctant engine, we were off again, this time bound for La Rochelle. The engine stopped off Port Navallo and we had a very quiet passage down the coast outside the Ile d'Yeu. According to the log, "we never actually lost steerage way".

At night, it was truly magical as we slipped smoothly along, trailing a glowing phosphorescent wake. Visibility was poor as we approached Pertuis d'Antioche so we sounded our way in and eventually moored alongside a French yacht in the outer harbour of La Rochelle, 39 hours out from the Morbihan, a distance of 131 miles.

We spent a day in La Rochelle shopping etc, and later on called in at the Yacht Club which was in the process of renovation.

The people there tried to discourage us from sailing on the Coureau d'Oléron and insisted that the Pertuis Mamusson was impassable. But one member was more constructive. I think he could see that we were reasonably experienced and, while stressing the need for caution, admitted that it was possible to get through.

June 14th was overcast with a light south-westerly wind when we slipped at midday. Outside, the visibility was poor and it seemed foolhardy to beat amongst the mud banks inside Oléron, so we went to St Martin, Ile de Ré instead.

The only drawback there was a number of smelly berths near the sewerage outflows! Still, we eventually found a good spot and enjoyed a walk around the ancient town and had a look at the old church which, it seemed, was still recovering from an English bombardment many years before! The basin was rather full of yachts and, moored in the middle, was an old tunnyman earning its keep as a crêperie. It looked forlorn, but I suppose it could have been left to rot somewhere, which would have been worse.

We had to lock out early next morning in a flat calm so we pleaded with the engine which surprised us by bursting into life. Just through La Pallice narrows the Anse d'Oubye looked rather fun so we approached gingerly, sounding our way in, and eventually anchoring for breakfast with a light 'picnic' anchor. It was here that Ian remarked "I never thought I'd have to use the lead because I really needed to". 'Swinging the lead' of course is hardly high on the modern Master Mariner's curriculum – but, I'm afraid, with no echo sounder there was simply no alternative.

Then we sailed to Ile d'Aix for lunch, having gone as far as we could until we touched bottom. Naturally, we were on a rising tide – and wanted to get reasonably close to the shore. It was still a long way off though, so we didn't land, and after lunch made our way towards La Charente. The visibility was good enough to make out the buoys and leading marks which duly appeared on cue. It was fascinating to cruise in such a low lying estuary with wooded hillocks in the hinterland.

The north bank was dotted with little fishing huts with large drop nets, each occupied by a fisherman and his family enjoying a Sunday picnic. On the other side cows grazed at the waters edge, and both banks were lined with tall, slender rushes with larks singing overhead. There's something rather magical about sailing right into the heart of the countryside.

There's a bridge above Soubise under which we expected, or rather hoped, to pass. It was false optimism! It failed to open, even though we could see a man in the control tower looking through his binoculars at us! We hung around hopefully for a bit, then turned back and tied up to a large black buoy. We later discovered that the bridge operator needed 24 hours notice before opening it. The tide was pretty strong but Ian managed to get ashore to sample the local cafés. I stayed on board and had a happy time trying to paint a picture of this pretty little red-roofed town with its houses clustered around the church on the hill. I was engrossed, listening to the whispering reeds and the chuckle of the water which gradually darkened as the light began to fade.

We drifted down river the following morning until we were met by fierce squalls and rain. We were a bit late on the tide and the bar looked distinctly rough so we turned round and had an exhilarating sail back, surging along at almost 7 knots. After lunch the wind dropped to about Force 3 or 4 so we set off through the Coureau d'Oléron again bound for the La Seudre river. It was exciting tacking through these tortuous channels which were somewhat casually buoyed. In fact, the whole place was a maze of withies marking oyster beds. Passing under the Great Oléron bridge, which dominates the whole stretch of water, was extremely alarming. We understood there was a minimum height of 15 metres and I kept saying to myself that 15 metres was 45 feet and that our mast was less than 40 feet, but I was still worried. When, at last, we found the right section, which was indicated by large red and green marks on the bridge itself, and finally shot underneath I felt a huge sense of relief. There was plenty of clearance as it happened but I still find bridges somewhat frightening.

Although the tide was well up we felt it wise to keep to the main channel. There were a whole load of small yellow conical buoys which weren't marked on the chart – and later learnt they'd been put there by oyster fishermen to keep ships off their beds. We were also warned not to ground on any oyster beds. I never understood whether they were worried that we might damage our boat on the concrete pens or damage their oysters. I suspect it was the latter because we subsequently heard some pretty horrifying tales of what fishermen did to anyone caught poaching them!

There were electricity cables across the entrance to La Seudre but we sailed safely under them and then entered the canal to Marennes sailing gently along with just the genoa. The place was a hive of activity with oysters everywhere. We tied up to a convenient looking wall about a mile below the town, but a friendly fisherman on a bicycle told us to go further up so, on we went, until we reached the lock gates. We were too late to enter so tied up to the west wall, which was studded with golden samphire and sea lavender.

We tied a masthead line to a convenient tree and were ashore in time for a meal at the Cheval Blanc. The following day we went into the basin and lay with an anchor from the bows and a stern line tied to some trees. The local yard gave us a nice wide plank for going ashore and were extremely friendly. Apparently, we were the first English yacht to visit them. They were so delighted to see us that they let us stay for nothing! The town itself was about 5 minutes away, and reached through attractive public gardens. From our berth, the elegant church steeple rising up out of the trees was a particularly impressive sight.

Marennes was a fascinating place and we stayed there for three enjoyable days, one of which Ian spent with a fisherman, Maurice Soutel, who took him to look at the Pertuis Mamusson. Ian was clearly impressed.

"There were great breaking seas right across the entrance, and pyramids of solid water leaping into the air", he said.

It was obviously a dangerous place and best avoided – whatever size of boat you had.

All in all then, he much enjoyed his day in spite of a rather extravagant breakfast of oysters and red wine which was taken at 0300.

The patron of the Cheval Blanc had provided him with a bottle of vin rouge, a loaf of bread and home-made paté, all of large dimensions, and much to his taste – completely free of charge. Maurice had brought the same, plus a sack of oysters, and in spite of having no common language, the two men had a wonderful day and came back the best of friends!

Later on we took a car trip to Brouage, an ancient port, but now a couple of miles inland.

We also visited Le Chapus which looked rather fun, but was too full of oyster boats to have much room for yachts. This part of the world was dominated by oysters – with dozen upon dozen of flat-bottomed oyster boats and little red-roofed oyster-fishermen's huts spread along the channels. Incidentally the Marennes oysters are world famous and particularly delicious.

The locals all warned us about Pertuis Mamusson, which, they said, should only be attempted in ideal conditions, which meant one hour before high water and with offshore winds. We met two fishermen who'd had near disasters there. The swell gets up so quickly and the breakers are charged with sand.

By June 20th we felt it was time to move on but the weather forecast was appalling so instead, we decided to go over to Le Tremblade which would mean sailing through considerably more sheltered waters. It rained, of course, but by 0825 we were tied up at a staging at the head of the canal and eating breakfast.

The Capitaine du Port had been most helpful, and even found a stake and drove it in for us to give us something to which we could attach a line from our masthead. Although the wind stayed strong, it was a fine day and Le Tremblade seemed a cheerful little place with good shops, a market and a super patisserie! In the bank we enquired about buses to Ronce les Bains, only to find we'd just missed the only one! Fortunately a woman overheard our conversation and offered to drive us over in the afternoon.

We gratefully accepted and had a most enjoyable trip. She even took us for a drive along the coast via the new 'Route Touristic' through pine forests and sand dunes to La Coubre lighthouse and the Côte Sauvage. This is a barren stretch of sand with ferociously heavy breakers. There were warnings in three languages against bathing but, it seemed, people regularly ignored them and sometimes lost their lives.

Our friend, Madam Bernard had a beautiful flower shop and her husband had a boatyard, and after drinks on board they took us ashore. Monsieur Bernard built proper wooden fishing boats and yachts, and fine vessels they looked too.

We got off next morning as soon as we floated. There was no wind and pouring rain. A light northerly wind greeted us when we got out of the canal, so did the sun.

We decided to have a look at the Pertuis Mamusson. There was quite a swell running and the area looked rather 'sullen'. As we beat slowly across the channel we passed a fisherman. Thinking he'd just come through, we asked him if it was OK. His reaction was ambivalent. "Possibly yes, possibly no," he explained. It was hardly encouraging. We also realised that we were running late and the tide, having turned, was now running west. Still, we sailed on up to Pte d'Arvert, but as the wind increased it was obvious we wouldn't make it that day. Shadows would appear on the horizon like islands, then suddenly dissolve into masses of white foam.

It was weird and rather alarming so we rounded Galen d'Or and sailed back along the northern channel, north of Bry bank, a dangerous quicksand! This southern shore of Oléron is wooded and it looked as if there were pretty little bays to anchor in, but unfortunately they all dry out so you really needed a centreboarder or a boat with twin keels.

We passed under the Great Oléron bridge again bound for Le Château. There was a fairly strong breeze and we raced up the channel but luckily, at the entrance, the wind eased and we sailed in more sedately, lowering the sails as we went. Friendly people helped us with our lines etc and soon we were tied up alongside lying comfortably in oozy soft mud.

We thought Le Château was extremely picturesque and the town, a mere 10 minute walk inland was a lively little holiday resort with decent shops. After that, we went on to La Cotinère where we tied up to the staging alongside the Hôtel de Bains.

The owner was very friendly and provided us with lots of local knowledge about La Cotinère where, although they were building a new breakwater, there was usually too much swell to lie alongside which is why the all the boats had legs and moored fore and aft. Legs were essential, he insisted.

Having studied the chart, we thought it might be amusing to have a look at Port de Douhet. There was a lovely stretch of reddish gold sands there backed by forest. As we approached, we could see a breakwater with a number of boats moored outside but no sign of a harbour – just a mole on the eastern side and what looked like broken masonry to the west with water breaking over it. With an onshore wind we decided to turn round and ran back to Boyardville where we enjoyed a wonderful supper!

Then we were homeward bound. We called in at La Rochelle again where we met Archie Black in *Black Jack*. He'd been exploring Coureau d'Oléron too so we compared notes.

Marans, just north of La Rochelle looked an interesting river to explore, so off we went. Again, the marks were rather sparse and their colours rarely agreed with the chart. A few scattered buoys marked the shoals on some of the bends, but in general we kept to the middle and hoped for the best! It reminded me of the River Parret up to Bridgewater. In fact I felt quite nostalgic meandering through flat countryside amongst the cows and sheep, then cruising through the tree-lined, reed-fringed canal past meadows and cornfields where corncrakes were croaking.

We found a good berth alongside a French yacht in the harbour. There were plenty of good shops at Marans which is on the main Nantes–Rochelle road. The lorries thundering past would be tiresome for the shopkeepers but it was peaceful enough where we were. We found a good quiet restaurant Hôtel des Voyageurs close to the boat and much better than it looked from the outside.

Next morning as we got to the open sea we ran into a Force 4 – 5 north-westerly dead on the nose and a choppy sea – which was depressing. We took down our sails and lunched in moderate comfort and discussed where to go next. I must say I was feeling rather despondent at the thought of a long plug to windward close hauled all night; I didn't admit it of course, but when Ian said "You know, Mum, it's not an endurance test," I was glad to agree, so we turned around and had a marvellous reach back to La Rochelle where we met up with Colonel Stevens of *Query* and spent an enjoyable evening together.

We spent the next few days sailing up the coast; sometimes with a fair wind, sometimes on a beat. We called at St Gilles-sur-Vie but the harbour was too shallow so were forced to go further up the river which was busy with yachts and holiday makers. Ian caught some mackerel for supper and drank his last can of beer as we reached Concarneau. This place, famous for its tunneymen had always sounded so fascinating but was rather disappointing. There were few fishermen and too many tourists and everything was terribly expensive.

We sailed across to the Baie de la Foret looking for a new marina. It was all a myth so we tied to a jetty there. It was a pretty estuary, but shallow with a narrow channel. We sailed around to Benodet under all the sails we could find, including a dinghy spinnaker. It must have looked odd!

This is where we met Mr Moore of *Golden Beaver* who kindly gave us instructions for his 'secret haven' the Anse de Toulven, which we visited that afternoon. It really was an enchanting little inlet, quiet and secluded and absolutely beautiful; just the sort of place we cruising people are always in search of. We'd have like to have spent longer there and taken more soundings. The chart suggested it dried completely, but Mr Moore disputed that and we reckoned there might be 4ft at L.W.S. at our particular anchorage. We motored down river again after tea and finished up at the Grand Hotel as Mr Moore's guests.

The following day, July 1st, we were off again in a fresh north-west wind. Rounding Pemarch it was infuriating to pass six yachts sailing south with their spinnakers set, while here we were struggling to make some northing! Still, the sun was out and we had a pleasant sail tacking close along the shore eventually anchoring in Audierne's outer harbour.

Then it was off again, setting course for La Vieille. I was determined to go through the Passe de Trouziard because my fellow original cadet member, John Morris had done it the previous year and honour was at stake! What a maze of rocks. At dead low water they looked slightly different from the ones in Adlard Cole's picture in the R.C.C. Journal. However, they sorted themselves out, and with a terrific swirl of tide, we shot through the gap like a champagne cork, Ian taking photos as we went.

It was hair-raising, but great fun and followed by a pleasant glow of satisfaction! Then on to Douarnenez indulging in a bit more rock dodging along the way. The town itself is about two miles from the Port de Plaisance, but there were fairly frequent buses.

We more or less drifted to l'Aberbenoit and were intrigued to see the peasants spreading seaweed from carts and horses on to their tiny patches of land reclaimed from gorse. We found a water tap labelled 'Eau potable. Interdit laver les voitures'. We supposed it meant we could drink it! A friendly native gave us a lift to the nearest restaurant, about a mile away, and after a simple meal we had a delightful walk back in the cool of a summer's evening through the quiet country lanes.

Time was getting on. It was now July 4th and I had an appointment on the 9th, so rather reluctantly we decided to miss the Scillies. Since we were nearly out of petrol we

decided to slip round to l'Abervrac'h before breakfast, but at
the entrance it was foggy with visibility about 10 yards, so
we returned back on course passing the wrong side of Mean
Rennet, then anchored for breakfast. The tide was now
running strongly out of l'Abervrac'h but the fog had cleared a
bit. As the tide was running hard we kept in as close as we
could to miss the worst of it. There were new pontoons at
l'Abervrac'h which made it easy to get ashore so we were
able to collect duty free, petrol and stores all in a quarter of
an hour.

Then off again, through the Malouine channel – with a big
sullen swell crashing against the rocks. Off Ile Vierge we set
course for Dartmouth and enjoyed a quiet uneventful
passage, mainly close hauled, in varying winds, and were
tied up in the marina just before midnight, 31½ hours out.
The following day was Sunday, July 6th which brought that
disastrous gale which caught so many yachtsmen out. How
lucky we were to be safely tied up in Dartmouth, our
favourite harbour.

We got back to Beaulieu on July 8th having spent a night
in Weymouth on the way. The only observation of note was
the exceptional visibility across West Bay. We could see the
whole coastline from Berry Head to Portland, something I'd
never experienced before.

So ended a truly wonderful cruise. I hope I never get too
old to lose that marvellous feeling of excitement when you
reach a new port. For me, a sense of adventure is
everything!

But back to the job in hand – and our passage to Porto
Calero. The night was clear but through the hours of
darkness the wind steadily increased so, by dawn, *Mary
Helen* was making more than six knots. By this time, the
seas were irregular with breaking crests many of which
came tumbling on board. During the day, things got steadily
worse. Water swept across the decks and the wind
increased in intensity. After rolling up the jib, we turned our

attention to the mainsail. Unfortunately the line which pulled the leech, or back end of the sail, down to the boom was too short; a serious oversight by the yard – which, in such difficult conditions, made a second reef almost impossible.

That left us with only one real alternative: to dispense with the mainsail altogether and continue under staysail alone. The main drawback was the direction of the wind which was well forward of the beam, so without sufficient drive, we made a great deal of leeway. On the other hand, it was considerably less stressful – though, with the odd sea or two crashing over the bows, we still got wet.

Incidentally, we found out later that the wind managed to blow at 35 knots for a period of twelve hours. No wonder it was just a little uncomfortable.

We continued with only the staysail all night. By dawn, the wind had eased to Force 4, from the east, which meant that, once again, we could hoist the reefed mainsail and jib. Our earlier antics had pushed us south of our rhumb line but during the day, we managed to claw our way back. Whilst the sun shone, there was still a haze about.

It might herald a sirocco which, in turn, could reduce visibility even further.

I sincerely hoped not.

As the wind freshened, *Mary Helen* picked up her skirts and flew along at close to her maximum speed. We rolled up the jib at dusk but had to make more ground along our rhumb line before bearing away to sail down the east coast of Lanzarote.

By midnight, it was really rough and dark. In the inky blackness we handed the mainsail, bore away, then gybed under staysail alone.

Under reduced canvas, we still managed about three knots, though without the steadying effect of the mainsail, the boat would roll fairly heavily from time to time – but at least we weren't being splattered by spray – and the leak had disappeared.

Lanzarote was to the west of us and, as we closed the coast, lights began to penetrate the haze.

It was comforting because, up until then, we'd not seen anything at all. Ponta Delgada light had probably been obscured by the murk – but the radar knew where we were, so, once again, I suppose technology triumphed.

After dawn, the wind eased and, with just the staysail up, we ran gently along the coast and past the airport. With the sun shining, it was such a contrast from the day before – and for that, all the more enjoyable.

We reached Porto Calero at 1415 on Sunday, October 8th 2000 and made fast to a pontoon at the western side of the entrance. Before long, our damp oilskins were hanging in the rigging while a canvas wind scoop fitted to the forehatch was directing air down below and helping to dry everything out. We'd experienced our first dusting and were glad to be in.

This particular trip had been a kind of shakedown cruise. As a result, there was a fair amount of work to be done. For a start, it was obvious that we needed another pump – preferably one which could be operated by the person on watch. We needed proper lazyjacks for the mainsail, decent fastenings for the forehatch and skylight, another block for the second reef and another copper anti-chafe sheet on the mast. Oh yes, and the staysail needed repairing too.

Track of *Mary Helen* in 1969
Coureau D'Oléron

Chapter Seven

LIFEBOAT TO *EMANUEL*

On October 17th my son Ian arrived aboard his 39-footer *Independent Freedom*, having sailed from Gibraltar before getting ready to cross the Atlantic on the last leg of his circumnavigation. It was an emotional family reunion – the boats also represented two generations, a case of the old meeting up with the new.

How wonderful that *Mary Helen* and *Independent Freedom* would be sailing to the Caribbean together.

Indeed, the event was hugely symbolic because Ian had been tracking an earlier passage made by my father who, in 1938, with my sister Marguerite as Mate, took *Caplin* half-way round the world. Their starting points were different of course; Ian bought his 39ft Bermudian schooner in New York, and set off from there – while my father's 30ft gaff yawl was based in Bridgewater. That apart, their journeys were essentially the same, so it was interesting to compare them – which is precisely what Ian set out to in his subsequent book *Sailing in Grandfather's Wake*.

Lanzarote itself was excellent. From our berth we could watch all the comings and goings; I developed a particular rapport with the crew of *The Yellow Submarine* which took a party of tourists out every day and showed them what life was like at the bottom of the sea. Later on, we went ourselves, and were absolutely overwhelmed by the experience. Watching such a wide variety of marine life at close quarters was simply unforgettable.

Donald's wife Lucy had come out with Teddy, their youngest son, during half-term, which added to the holiday atmosphere. Donald and Teddy slept aboard *Independent Freedom*; Lucy joined me on *Mary Helen*.

The next few days were spent sightseeing; we saw just about all there was to see.

Lanzarote is another island of contrasts, with fertile agricultural land to the north-east and volcanic desolation to the south-west – though even here, in one of the valleys, vines have been planted and seem to flourish. We also came across a restaurant perched on a volcano where they use natural heat, which rises up from just below the surface, to cook the food.

When the family finally left, and after all the jobs had been successfully completed, we left Porto Calero on Saturday, October 28th bound for La Gomera. The swell was moderate, and so was the wind: a benevolent Force 4 from the north-east.

Ian saw us off and would follow in a few days time.

We anchored at Papogoya at the southern end of Lanzarote where we had supper before leaving at 2200 hours. Once clear of the land, *Mary Helen* surged ahead under mainsail and staysail – beneath a virtually cloudless sky.

By 0800 the following day, the wind was a good Force 5 or 6 from the north-east, which was the cue to reduce sail. Both reefs were taken in this time – but even then, *Mary Helen* was still sailing fast. It was great while it lasted but by the afternoon the wind had increased; the sea was much bigger too, and the boom was frequently dipping in the water. At dusk, as we picked out the lights of Grand Canary and Tenerife, the wind grew even stronger – putting yet more pressure on poor *Mary Helen*, so, at 2200, we handed the mainsail. The seas between the swell were short, steep – and, on occasion, sufficiently energetic to find their way on board, so we were shipping quite a lot of water.

As the night wore on, the wind increased – so did the seas. With only the staysail up, *Mary Helen* still managed 6½ knots – and by the time we reached the south-eastern end of Tenerife – was charging her way through enormous, breaking waves.

As the storm screeched and howled she started shipping water. Her speed was now approaching 7 knots, the wind was Force 8 to 9 from the north-east and we were pumping every four hours.

It was slightly alarming – but I was used to heavy weather.

I remembered a particularly difficult trip on *Emanuel* with my father. I was only eighteen years old and the boat was hurtling along, under full main, off the coast of North Cornwall. It was teaming with rain, visibility was minimal and I was wrestling with the tiller, trying hard to hold her on course. Dad told me to gybe to avoid some rocks, then steer as near north as possible while he shortened sail. He put four rolls in the main and dropped the staysail – by which time we had a full-blown gale on our hands. The seas were so big that Dad insisted on tying a line round me; there were no such things as harnesses in those days! To be honest, I found it all rather exhilarating, though fearfully wet.

I remember it all so clearly; as conditions improved for a moment, we managed to get round Trevose – and catch sight of Padstow just a couple of miles to windward.

Then, fortuitously, the wind suddenly veered to west-south-west – which meant we could clear the land in a single tack. Passing Stepper Point was more difficult and had us short-tacking to keep in the narrow channel. There was even a notice with the simple message 'Keep Close to this Point' – so we did.

We missed stays once when the jib fouled the forestay which caused much consternation. Dad couldn't bear the thought of coming in under the eyes of the coastguard in such a slovenly state so he hoisted the staysail and started to lower the jib which promptly fouled about half-way down just as I put her about. Naturally, with the jib backed, we lost precious momentum, so Dad clawed it down, and, at last, slowly but surely, round we came, with *Emanuel*'s bowsprit almost hanging over the rocks. Of course, we felt mighty relieved, until, with a bump, she touched bottom. We'd held on too long and should have tacked back again. I frantically pushed the tiller and hoped. She hesitated for a moment, then, off she came, churning out sand as she ploughed her way free. Then another shudder. Had we grounded again?

Dad thought not and tried to reassure me. Apparently there was no immediate danger to life or limb, he explained. Which was strangely unsettling. Until then, the thought had never occurred to me.

We anchored off Hawkes Cove, a little astern of the lifeboat and started clearing up. The saloon was a mess – with gear and equipment everywhere – and a fair bit of water, but in the end we got straight again and after a proper cooked breakfast felt almost back to normal. As a bonus, the rain had stopped and the sun was trying hard to break through so we were reasonably optimistic. But then we looked at the barometer.

It was down to 28.79 and still falling. The wind too was still at gale force and I could tell that Dad was worried. As a precaution, we prepared the kedge so we could let it go if the bower anchor dragged. We also slid a weight down the cable to reduce snubbing – and let out all 30 fathoms. Dad even put extra lashings on the mainsail to reduce windage.

As the tide rose, we lay beam on to the seas which produced such a horribly uncomfortable motion that I decided to stay on deck. Astern lay the subtly-named Doom Bar and Hell's Bay – which was hardly comforting; on the other hand, the view was magnificent.

In a gale like that, with no engine, laying a kedge to windward would have been just about impossible – but I was still relatively unconcerned. It never occurred to me that the cable could break – and since we weren't dragging I wasn't worried at all – more frustrated that I couldn't go ashore and stretch my legs.

Dad, in contrast, was extremely anxious – though he only told me later. He was also making plans to take us both off in the dinghy – when he noticed the coastguards signalling. Having forgotten his semaphore, he got me to flash a message in Morse. They were worried about the falling tide which, they said would leave us aground at low water. We knew that wasn't true but appreciated their concern and asked them if they might use one of the local fishing boats hauled up on the beach to bring us ashore. They made a counter-suggestion: why not call out the lifeboat? It sounded splendid to me but Dad was less keen. However, thirty minutes later we saw the crew hurrying across the fields. In hardly any time at all, they were manoeuvring their well-equipped vessel alongside, taking *Emanuel* in tow and moving us into deeper water 50 yards further on. Dad then dropped both anchors while the crew took a line ashore. After that, although the glass fell to 28.50, we slept like babies – and since then, I've always supported the R.N.L.I.

As I say, it was exciting stuff, but I never felt truly frightened, largely, I suppose because I had faith in the boat and her skipper – but also because to be anything other than optimistic would only make matters worse.

And so it was now, all these years later. I felt uncomfortable but simply accepted it. However prudent you are, there are times when heavy weather is unavoidable and you just have to put up with it.

Anyhow, at dawn, we began rounding Pta Rasca. The wind eased a little then suddenly disappeared – but as the heavy, north-westerly swell collided with the north-easterly current, the motion was awkward to say the least.

Without so much as a whisper, we motor-sailed towards La Gomera running into strong winds and a powerful current some five miles off – but arrived at 1245.

Another test was over and *Mary Helen* had passed. All the modifications carried out in Lanzarote had stood up well and we were ready for the big one.

Ian arrived in *Independent Freedom* on Sunday November 5th after a fast passage and our thoughts turned to the final preparations. We had a passage plan; weather charts were studied on a daily basis. With a front on the way though, we decided to take some time off and explore.

The island is full of contrasts. To the south all you see are steep, arid slopes.

Then, near the top of the mountains, everything changes. The landscape is lush, with rich, green grass and dense native Mediterranean forest. The views – of the shimmering sea and deep calderas – were spectacular. I felt inspired.

I wanted to spread my wings.

Chapter Eight

WAR YEARS. MICE LIKE ROPES

I was impatient and ready for the big adventure. I'm not very good at waiting.

I like action. So do boats; they want to be used. Of course, sometimes, you have to be patient. We had no choice during the Second World War – when poor *Mary Helen* was laid up in a creek on the beautiful Beaulieu River. As a precaution, I recall, we removed most of her gear and stored it in a barn which belonged to George Brown, the local farmer. It was six long years before we could think about sailing her again though, by then, mice had munched their way through all our neatly coiled ropes and *Mary Helen*'s transom had opened up rather badly and would have to be renewed. But she was still basically sound.

Funnily enough however, I remember receiving a letter from a complete stranger around about that time. What a pity that such a pretty little boat should fall into disrepair, he wrote, suggesting we hand her over to him before she fell apart completely.

I was furious and wanted to dash off a suitably angry reply but was persuaded that a cold, stony silence would be far more insulting. In the end John sailed her back to Dorset with a friend.

John was working for Jack Laurent Giles during the War while I did some of their typing. They were designing boats for the Navy and it was all very hush hush. Anyhow, I was firmly told not to ask any questions. Then Jack went up to London and John took over Newman's yard in Poole.

I was sent home to my parents where I did a short stint of teaching at our village school. Then John found a house to rent in Lilliput, on the banks of Poole harbour.

It was a necessary move as we were starting a family. Donald duly arrived and what with rations, coupons and a new baby, life was hectic.

Somehow, during the War you felt guilty if you weren't actively involved. I was lucky enough to have some domestic help so I used to spend the mornings teaching maths at a local school. We were involved in 'fire watching' duties which meant many sleepless nights. There was a decoy set up in an old ruined village on Brownsea Island to confuse the enemy and one night during a raid there were aeroplanes buzzing around the harbour. One flew right in front of our house and I could have shot it down if only I'd had a gun!

When the boats that John was building were completed, the Admiralty sent the skippers down for final tests etc, and we used to look after them. Many were from overseas and it was interesting, though hardly surprising to see how much bigger the Americans rations were than ours. I'll never forget one of them bringing us a 7lb tin of demerara sugar! I also remember a young Australian who asked me if he could watch me bathing Donald. He had a son of the same age but had never seen him.

Ian arrived in 1943, Edward in 1944. Malcolm delayed his appearance until 1947 when an elderly relative of John's said, "You should call him Victor my dear".

We had other ideas. Since I'd had to miss an R.C.C. committee meeting on his account we christened him Malcolm Roger Norman after the three current flag officers!

Actually, Malcolm is probably the youngest ocean racer. We were racing with friends on the Dinard Race when he was minus three months! His first words were 'lee oh'. We'd been sailing in Poole harbour and were beating up one of the narrow channels with Malcolm wedged in his carry cot on a saloon bunk. Every time we tacked, he was tipped from side to side. The following morning we heard a little voice softly singing "lee oh, lee oh" in the nursery.

We had a dinghy on the beach and when Donald was two we signed him on as a Poole fisherman so we could take him sailing. It was inevitable that they should all become sailors, though I remember when I scolded him for some minor misdemeanour he replied, "All right then Mummy, I won't like sailing". It was the worst thing he could think off – but, of course, it was he who sailed across the Atlantic with me more than fifty years later!

So, as I say, it wasn't until 1946 that *Mary Helen* was ready for sea again. After such a long interlude, I was too; more than ready. After spending a couple of hectic days shutting up the house, buying provisions and ferrying the children (complete with ration cards) to my mother's, we left Poole on August 1st at 1830 bound for Cherbourg. It was wonderful to get away and we gently slid through the night with the yankee set as a spinnaker.

Suddenly, at 0700, with *Mary Helen* making about 3 knots, I heard a huge, almighty thump by the bow. For a moment I thought it was a mine! I'm not usually dramatic but with thoughts of the War still fresh in my mind I suppose it was understandable. In fact it was a log, more like a tree-trunk really, but fortunately *Mary Helen* had merely shoved it unceremoniously aside. Nevertheless, for once, I felt slightly unnerved and when the wind freshened and I went below, I was seasick. As I say, quite uncharacteristic.

To shake myself out of it I went up on deck and felt very much better. We were well reefed down but making good progress – until the rain came and visibility dropped to about two miles. We hoped our Dead Reckoning was right because the tide was about to turn. If it set us further west than we'd planned, trying to beat back against it in such a strong easterly wind would be hopeless.

Fortunately, at 1600, we picked out Cherbourg breakwater.

The rest of our cruise was spent picking up the threads and visiting old haunts – but the place that still sticks in my mind is St Malo. The centre of the town was vandalised after most of France had been liberated and the sheer scale of the devastation had a profoundly dramatic effect on me. Before the War, we felt safe, secure – and part of the civilised world. Afterwards, things were less predictable. Above all though, it was good to be back on the water. Sailing in general, and cruising in particular, gives you a feeling of freedom like nothing else I know.

Now though, perched on the edge of the Atlantic, the waiting was just about over.

As countdown approached, we checked and rechecked the gear, then stowed some last minute stores including a selection of locally bought fruit.

The atmosphere was exciting but poignant as well. After all, John designed her with the idea of crossing the Atlantic. It goes without saying that we would have done the trip together, the two of us, but here I was, aboard our brave little ship setting off without him. I wondered what he might have thought about that. Curiously, I sometimes found myself calling Donald 'John' – which shows that memories never die. It was a bit eerie though.

I knew how *I* felt. I was proud of *Mary Helen* and proud of John. I also wanted to fulfill my life-long ambition and expunge once and for all that poisonous sense of disappointment which affected me so deeply when my father set sail alone in 1934. Being left behind is like being left out – or even rejected – which, in turn, leaves an enduring sense of sadness. I'm not normally given to introspection; I much prefer to find practical ways of putting things right. This would be my way of putting things right.

And so, on Wednesday, November 8th 2000, we took a final look at the weather charts while the harbourmaster ran a prediction on his computer. The nearby low, which had brought with it such high winds, seemed to be moving away to the north-east.

There was no guarantee but we still decided to leave. So that was that. We left San Sebastian at 1025 in company with *Independent Freedom.* The plan was to sail south for about three days to about 21°N 25.5°W before turning west. Our destination was St Lucia – although at one stage we thought about the Cape Verde Islands. In the end though, we both felt it might be better to crack on rather than stopping en route.

That day, as we sailed down the coast of La Gomera with Ian, the wind was all over the place. Eventually the breeze wandered off altogether so we motored a bit to see if we could find it.

The sea was confused with a huge swell and vicious cross-current which made life difficult – but at least the sun shone during the day and the moon kept us company at night. We also still had Ian – but not for very much longer. He radioed just after dark to tell us that both his sails had torn and that *Independent Freedom* would be making for the Cape Verde Islands. We thought we might follow, but events would overtake us.

We were making slow progress, and the light wind backed so much that eventually we had to gybe. That proved disastrous. As the boom swung across, the gooseneck failed. It simply snapped in two. Donald examined it carefully, looked up, and gave it to me straight.

"We're in serious trouble, Mother," he said.

It was awful. A cutter without a mainsail is a potential cripple.

We dropped the main and took stock. Since it was too rough to turn back and unlikely that the Cape Verdes would have adequate repair facilities, there was really only one way out. We had to carry on. But with no mainsail, we

wouldn't beat any records. Never mind; we still had three
headsails and plenty of water and food.

It was time to get going again so we set the yankee and
staysail – both of which were boomed out to give us as
much drive as possible. In the light breeze however, we just
crawled along; Hierro was in sight all day. Fortunately, that
evening the wind increased to Force 3 from north-north-east
and we gently picked up speed. At midnight we set the
yankee to port.

Next day, the wind backed to north-west by west and fell
light. It was agonising; how we needed that mainsail!

On Sunday, November 11th, we watched the clouds
building ominously above, so handed the yankee in case of
a squall. As it happened, the wind failed completely!

This was no way to cross the Atlantic and we knew it. So,
ever the optimist, I cheerfully suggested lashing the boom to
the mast instead.

Donald was doubtful but agreed to give it a go and
promptly set to work. It took him two hours. At 1000 we
hoisted the main and it seemed OK. With a light breeze
coming in from the north-west, we could only make a course
of 190°; as dark, heavy rain clouds assembled, we prepared
to get wet. By the afternoon, we were treated to intermittent
showers before the wind suddenly freed and flexed its
muscles. This was more like it. Not only were we making 5½
knots; we were also sailing in the right direction!

It only lasted for about half an hour before disappearing
completely, leaving us utterly becalmed. We were suddenly
motionless in the middle of the ocean.

We stayed like that until midnight when the faintest of
zephyrs turned up from the north-west. We were moving
again – but only just.

By the afternoon it was strong enough to push us along at
4½ knots and by evening the seas had started to build. As
night fell, the clouds organised themselves into huge,
dramatic shapes, like cosmic paintings. One looked like an

eagle – immense, open-winged and brilliant in the light of the moon. We were now below 25°N and nearing the Trades.

In the early hours of Monday, November 13th a large bulk carrier came a bit too close for comfort. Donald called her up and received necessary reassurances. She was probably further away than she looked but, silhouetted by the moon, her huge frothing bow wave glistening ahead of her, she made us feel tiny, fragile and vulnerable, so it was good to know that someone was watching out. They asked us who we were and where we were going.

"*Mary Helen*, on passage to the West Indies," we told them.

"Good luck and fair winds," he replied as if he really meant it. The radio operator, who had a slight accent – Dutch or Norwegian, I thought – sounded so encouraging that I wanted to meet him and see what he looked like.

With the wind a robust Force 5 from the north-east, and sailing with a double reefed mainsail and boomed out staysail, our daily runs were building steadily. Though the sea was moderate, thanks to a swell from north by west, the motion would best be described as lively. More importantly however, we were making good progress south, before turning west, and our little boat was moving eagerly across the endlessly heaving water.

On Wednesday, November 15th, we ticked off a week at sea. Our four-hours-on, four-hours-off routine was now a matter of routine as we prepared to alter course and embark on the crossing proper. So, at noon in position 22°40'N, 24°38.5'W *Mary Helen* turned her face towards the west, steering 270°.

The manoeuvre was followed by another good day's run which made us feel even better; morale was high. This was rollicking stuff. The boom, scraping the sea from time to time, picked up water in the mainsail and dumped it back in our laps as *Mary Helen* rolled upright; wave tops sloshed over the starboard quarter into the cockpit – and with so much spray flying about we could only open the forehatch for short periods during the day.

That night, the clouds made more pictures. There were birds, animals and an eerie Halloween mask with moonlight shining through the eyes.

The following day the wind veered to the south-east. It was still averaging about Force 5 but was stronger in the squalls. In the evening, under threatening black clouds, we dropped the mainsail and continued under staysail alone.

Conditions worsened during the night, with heavy prolonged rain and an angry Force 7 wind from east-south-east. The seas were vicious too – big, steep and breaking, they came crashing on board soaking everything in sight. We put the GPS in a tin box to protect it from lightning, and hung on grimly as *Mary Helen* rolled heavily. It was like a masochistic ride in a fun fair. It went on for the next forty-eight hours – but even with only one sail up, we still managed over 100 miles a day. To increase our discomfort, a large cross-swell had appeared which added a corkscrew motion to our bone-crushing gyrations and made it even easier to scoop up dollops of cold Atlantic Ocean. Sometimes the cockpit was flooded but with three pumps we soon sent everything back where it belonged.

As for *Mary Helen* herself, she simply took everything in her stride. I particularly enjoyed watching her rise up over the deep blue ocean, waggle her tail at the top of a wave, then swoop down the other side. Isn't it amazing how the really big ones don't always get you, while the more innocuous ones so often do?

Only late in the morning of Saturday November 18th did we get a glimpse of the sun when the rain eventually stopped. On the following day we also set the jib and continued at just over 4 knots.

Conditions remained much the same for a week, but on Saturday November 25th, the clouds became light and puffy as we entered the Trades. The sun too had altered character and was beaming benignly. To complete the change of mood, the wind eased to Force 4, east-north-east, and we saw our first flying fish. We were still rolling heavily but things were so vastly improved that it hardly seemed to matter.

To add to my sense of calm and wonder, I made a friend. In the early morning, and out of the blue, came a beautiful white coloured bird. He had a long feathery tail and a touch of yellow under the beak but at that time I had no idea what he was. He circled round *Mary Helen*, carefully inspecting us with his big brown eyes, then flew off.

Moments later, he returned for another look – as if making doubly sure that everything was OK. Quite illogically, I felt strangely exhaulted. It was if our guardian angel was looking after us. Thumbing through my books later on, I identified him as a long-tailed Tropic bird. After that, sailing through several pods of dolphins, and watching them play, only added to the sense of magic.

For the next few days the winds increased a little, then eased. The sea was moderate but the cross-swell remained, as we continued our way westward.

Occasionally, we took one over the stern, but pumping was still part of the daily routine so we took it in our stride. Having said that, we were shifting about 1½ buckets every four hours, which was probably slightly more than it should have been. Still, there was no sign of a major leak, as long as it didn't get worse, it was nothing to worry about.

The flying fish were still flying but none landed on deck. Pity!

Friday December 1st was a special day. It was the first time we took off our oilskins. The wind had eased to Force 2 to 3 from the south-east and we hoisted the yankee instead of the jib which gave us an extra shove. Things were getting better.

We handed the yankee on Sunday December 3rd which was timely because the halyard had badly chafed at the masthead. At noon we realised there were just 150 miles to go. In a gentle breeze and a moderate swell we were making extremely good progress and felt incredibly happy.

On Monday December 4th, dawn broke with a flourish. Strong colours streaked the sky, teasing the clouds with soft, pastel pink light. It would be our last such day totally surrounded by sea, so we prepared for the following day's landfall. Anchor chain was broken out, flags made ready and the radar positioned strategically on the bridgedeck. We then scrubbed and cleaned and tidied so *Mary Helen* looked her best.

Finally, in the early hours of Tuesday, December 5th lights appeared up ahead...

Chapter Nine

AT LAST, ALL BLIGHTS FORGIVEN

Dawn broke and ahead of us lay Antigua. Donald gave a shout and called me up on deck so I could see for myself. I was overwhelmed with relief. It was an emotional moment for both of us and felt like a dream.

"Are we really there?" I asked Donald.

"Actually, not quite, Mother dear," he replied with a grin, *"we still have about seven miles to go!"*

Donald had been here some forty years earlier with Lord Riverdale aboard *Bluebird of Thorne*, which I understand was the world's first proper twin keeled yacht. Anyhow, he certainly knew all the landmarks. We sailed leisurely past the Pillars of Hercules that mark the entrance to English Harbour then handed our two faithful headsails as we motored past Berkeley Point towards the dockyard.

The place was bursting with boats of every size and description but, at 1015 December 5th 2000, 26 days, 23 hours and 50 minutes after leaving La Gomera we managed to find a mooring off the Admiral's Inn.

We felt like conquerors. After savouring the moment I asked Donald to pass me the logbook and wrote five simple words which meant so much to me: 'At last, all blights forgiven'.

This was the end of a journey, not just to the West Indies but one which really began sixty-six years earlier when my father refused to take me across the Atlantic. After sailing so far on *Emanuel* and spending so much time together, his decision had left me numb. He knew how much I wanted to go and how much it meant to me – but still went ahead on his own. At the time it seemed like betrayal – which, I suppose, may sound extreme or even harsh – but I can only describe how I felt. Now though, as I sat in *Mary Helen*'s cockpit I felt nothing but pride, satisfaction – and forgiveness.

The following day, we had *Mary Helen* hauled out. The bottom was remarkably clean but some of the seams were damp so we had them recaulked.

It was only then that we heard about Ian. Apparently *Independent Freedom* had arrived in Jolly Bay just one day ahead of us – so we hired a car and braved the primitive Antigua roads to go and see him.

There was so much to talk about – but above all, we wanted to compare notes and check our noon positions. Amazingly, on November 29th we were within a mere ten miles of each other without knowing it – and all that after a chapter of accidents: what with Ian's damaged sails and our broken gooseneck, it was a most happy coincidence that both parties had decided against St Lucia and headed for Antigua instead.

What better place, and what better way to celebrate Christmas! With *Mary Helen* ashore, Donald insisted that, for safety's sake, I slept on *Independent Freedom* but once the repairs had been completed I moved back on board. Soon after that, the family flew out to join us, so, we moved *Mary Helen* round to Jolly Bay where we rented a villa with a quay for the two boats – and everyone was reunited.

The only drawback was the weather which was rather windy. Having said that, it was wonderfully warm – and Boxing Day, when we sailed the two boats round to Deep Bay and back, was just about perfect.

Having everyone together like this took me back to a time before the War when Dad thought it might be a nice idea to have a proper family holiday. After all, while we'd been off sailing, Mum had always been left behind to run the farm and look after the younger ones. She'd also just acquired a caravan. I've often wondered whether she bought it to have something of her own. Dad had his boat; she had her caravan.

Anyway, it was decided that she should take the 'kids' – as my brother and I used to call them – up to Scotland in it, while Dad and I went in *Emanuel*. It also provided the perfect opportunity to circumnavigate Britain.

We attended the R.C.C. meet in the Beaulieu River which, as usual, was tremendous fun. After a super party on board, we sailed down river in a fresh westerly wind with lots of people on boats cheering us as we passed. One hailed us with the latest weather forecast which we'd deliberately missed. In the event, their well intentioned warning of an impending gale came rather too late; we were off! Actually, our sail along the South Coast was pretty hectic and it was jolly hard work steering. A couple of hours on the tiller was more than enough. My arms got stiff and my fingers grew numb; even Dad thought it pretty strenuous and insisted I put on a lifeline, so I said, if that were the case, he would have to wear one as well. We then made a ship's rule that if only one of us were on deck in rough weather, a lifeline was *de rigueur*.

It was all most exhilarating. We were sailing at almost maximum speed – and although the log only gave us 6 knots we reckoned we must have been doing at least 7, since every now and then the log's rotor broke surface, so it must have been under-reading. Neither of us got very much sleep; the motion was far too violent. At daybreak we were surrounded by extremely thick fog, but by 0600 it cleared just enough for us to pick out the white cliffs of Beachy Head about a mile off. Seeing that famous landmark was quite a moment for me, I must say. With the wind and sea increasing, Dad rolled up the jib, we hove-to, then tied a fourth reef in the mainsail.

It was boisterous stuff; passing close to the Royal Sovereign Light Vessel, we could see the crew looked pretty uncomfortable too.

It was now a dead run for Dungeness, but we were worried about the danger of an uncontrolled gybe so thought it safer to approach it on a broad reach. We still had to gybe of course but at least, this way we could decide precisely when.

Although Dad had made coffee and soup during the night, neither of us felt like cooking a proper breakfast, so we made do with cold beef and bread and butter!

In spite of everything, Dad did gybe once by mistake. Luckily though the boom was at a reasonably modest angle and the mainsheet was fairly taut so no damage was done. Imagine how glad I was it was him, and not me! Even now, I still feel slightly anxious when running in rough seas.

Although we kept fairly close inshore, I thought the seas were huge, particularly off Dover. According to Dad's notes in the log however, they were only 'fairly big'. Thankfully, *Emanuel* was a jolly good sea boat and lifted safely to ride each overtaking wave. Nevertheless, we took quite a few breaking crests over the cockpit, and a good deal of water made its way below. By 1550 South Foreland was abeam. After that we had shelter from a weather shore. What a relief to be sailing in smoother water. We steered for Ramsgate and I began dreaming of a meal ashore and a good night's sleep. Some hope; Dad thought it a pity to waste such a super fair wind. He was right, of course, and I suppose I really agreed with him. For ships without engines a fair wind is an absolute gift, so I didn't argue. Anyway, we had plenty of grub and I wasn't really tired. Since the morning gale warning had only referred to an area as far east as the Dover Straits – and because the glass was beginning to rise – we decided to carry on and have some light refreshments. Dad always insisted on afternoon tea, usually with toast.

By 1530, with the wind still a fresh Force 5 – 6, the Kentish Knock Light Vessel came into view. Then, suddenly, without warning, a fierce squall descended. At the same moment we heard a loud bang aloft. Naturally, we thought it had to be the mast, but everything seemed OK. Dad bore away to ease the strain on the jib and called me up from below. Standing at the helm, I watched him going forward to check for signs of damage. He found nothing other than the fact that the lee rigging seemed rather slack. Clearly worried, he rolled up the jib and tightened the runners, then put her back on the right course. After that he went below and studied the charts to see where we might end up if the mast collapsed and we started to drift. I'd given up worrying by that time, and was perfectly confident that Dad would cope. I didn't imagine that the mast would go, and instead, simply thought the noise we heard was wind rattling about in the rigging!

The weather was still pretty wild and wet, but with five rolls in the mainsail and the reefed staysail we battled on. Eventually Dad let her forereach to the north-east, towards a reasonably uncluttered stretch of water. We had a tinned stew for supper after which I took over with instructions to call Dad when I could no longer keep awake. I lasted a couple of hours, then at 0030 on August 1st, I called him up. Cold, wet and tired, I was jolly glad to get below and was soon asleep. It takes a lot to keep me awake! When I woke up at first light I managed to scramble some eggs which we ate with spoons straight from the saucepan. The wind had eased a bit, so when we sighted Lowestoft we decided to go in – and finally entered the harbour at 1115.

A couple of friendly locals helped us tie up in the yacht basin.

Dad got a shipwright to come and look at the mast, but the man could find nothing wrong. He did however draw our attention to rather a lot of knots at the top, one of which might have worked a bit and made the noise. I still maintained it was only the sound of the storm! It was certainly blowy and once ashore, we had it confirmed that the wind had reached gale Force 8, so little *Emanuel* had done really well. The Royal Norfolk and Suffolk Yacht Club kindly made us honorary members on the strength of it and we dined there in the evening; luckily our best clothes had remained dry!

Talk about contrasts! Next day the wind was gone completely, and by the time various odd jobs had been done, it wasn't worth trying to leave. We did manage to get away on August 3rd. At first, the wind was light and from the north, then in the evening a light southerly arrived so we set the spinnaker. At least we had steerage way.

Most of that night the wind was variable. Sometimes we drifted and sometimes we sailed. At one point we even managed the breathtaking speed of two knots. By noon on August 4th we clocked up a good 40 miles and were close to the Cromer Light Vessel. There was almost no wind, so we launched the dinghy and I rowed across with some magazines. Well, someone told us they occasionally ran out of reading matter. Anyway I felt very important and the crew seemed to be pleased to see me.

I think they were somewhat surprised to see a girl and even gave me some letters to post. I don't expect many girls have acted as a light vessel postman! The next few days saw mostly light variable winds and at 0830 on August 7th we entered Fraserburgh harbour. We were 342 miles from Lowestoft, having just heard a weather forecast which promised imminent gales! We had a day ashore for shopping and were jolly glad to be safely in harbour because the bad weather duly arrived.

The port had seemed rather empty, but during the morning hundreds of drifters came in. It seemed that the recent spell of fair weather had kept the herrings low, but the bad weather had bought them up again, and since this was the first good catch of the season, prices were high. They told us we'd bought them luck, and the grocer gave me a box of chocolates! Lovely!

On August 9th we slipped away at 1100 but I ha[d] *Emanuel* with the dinghy because there was no win[d] inner harbour. There was plenty of wind outside thoug[h] we had to reef and hoist the smaller jib. I was feeling pleased with myself because by the time Dad cam[e] relieve me in the morning I'd fixed our position at 12 [m] South of Duncansby Head, and he said I was right! At 1[?] we anchored in Freswick Bay, the last stopover befo[re] rounding the Duncansby en route to the Pentland Firth. It [was] important to get the tide right for rounding the headland so[,] by 0230 we were off again and soon beating round Duncansby Head in a light west wind before anchoring off Scrabster to wait for the tide. By the afternoon the wind had gone northerly so we could up anchor, set sail and continue on the right course.

We had a lovely sail along that northern coast. It was curious to think that the whole of Britain lay behind that coast on our left; the scenery was spectacular too, with mountain ranges silhouetted against the sky. The night was a bit chilly though – which called for an extra jersey!

At 0700 on August 12th we were becalmed off Cape Wrath. It's an imposing headland and of course another turning point. Progress was rather slow as we rounded the point so we went into Loch Inchard, and anchored at 0730. There's a hotel mentioned in the Clyde Cruising Club handbook, but at that time it was a police station.

We managed to get some milk at a cottage, but that was all. Gradually we crept south, sometimes sailing, sometimes drifting; we even had the sweep out to keep us off the rocks at one point.

By 1630 on August 16th we anchored at Ullapool, just off the pier, and within an hour were amazed to see Mum's little car towing the caravan along the road overlooking the harbour. What fantastic timing; we'd sailed 750 miles and they'd motored 1000. We then enjoyed about ten days sailing and motoring with the family and pottering about down to Loch Duich which Mum eventually used as a base.

ly we 'children' thought we'd give the
mselves so went off in the car to Skye
great fun and a pity because we didn't
explore in greater detail. The scenery,
Cuillin Hills, is absolutely superb.

we saw the family off from Loch Duich,
were on our own again. There wasn't much
sailed across to Kyle Akin where we spent
woke to rain and a strong south-east wind but
n it was much calmer, so we weighed anchor.

dal stream through Kyle Rhea was fearsome and
us through at great speed; quite hair raising! Though
sea was essentially smooth there were several violent
dies. In Sleat Sound the wind failed about two miles north-
east of Sandaig and what with the pouring rain, it was all a
bit depressing. Later in the afternoon when the tide would be
against us, we managed to drift close to the east shore, and
anchored with the kedge about 50 yards off and quite close
to a spectacular waterfall, near a huge clump of white
heather. I rowed ashore and picked a bit but Dad was
reluctant to leave the ship lying in such an exposed
anchorage.

The calm held and we put out a fishing line, more in hope
than expectation. The nine o'clock weather forecast talked of
light easterly winds but Dad must have been worried
because he insisted on keeping an anchor watch which I
thought rather unnecessary. Still, he gave me a choice, so I
chose the first watch, which meant I could listen to Fecamp
radio! It was about 2230 when Dad turned in but he didn't
undress in case we needed to move. We had a candle lit on
the cabin table and after about half an hour it suddenly
flickered and went out. Naturally, I leapt up on deck and lo
and behold – the wind had arrived from the south-west. I
called Dad who was fast asleep. He woke up at once, and
with the wind freshening, we got underway. There was a
large dogfish struggling on the line, but we simply chucked it
in the dinghy, hoisted the sails and weighed the anchor!

The wind was increasing all the time and it was now pouring with rain. Luckily we got off on the right tack and were soon approaching the opposite side. We were obviously overcanvassed and as soon as we tacked Dad put several rolls in the mainsail. It was then that I remembered leaving the cabin porthole open so I leapt below and shut it. Fortunately nothing much had come in.

It was pitch dark and we were almost blinded by torrential rain as we tacked to and fro across the Sound. We more or less had to guess when to go about which was really rather exciting! Between tacks Dad managed to clean up a bit forward, shoving the kedge warp into the cabin and getting a bit of a reef in the staysail though there was no time to tie the points. The Sound was about a mile wide and we were both needed aft because I couldn't steer and keep a lookout as well. It had increased to a full gale by this time and the sea was getting rough. Since the tide was pouring through the narrow strait of Kyle Rhea, we couldn't turn and run back and even if we'd survived the overfalls, we couldn't have stemmed the 7 knot current. I was steering while Dad did the donkey work. At one point he pulled the jib sheet in too soon, so we missed stays but she soon gathered way again and round she came. Phew; that was some moment! The dinghy was struggling astern and slowing us down. Dad was also concerned that the painter might part. Fortunately it was fairly new and stayed in one piece. Sometimes the squalls were so fierce that we had to luff, but a drop in speed would have been disastrous so we dared not reduce sail. At last we weathered Sandraig, then picked up the two lights of Ornsay, before spotting a break in the land that must have been the entrance to Loch Nadal.

Dad was worried about the Fork Rocks, but we sailed safely past them! Looking at the chart before we went, it all looked so easy, but at the time, blinded by stinging rain and tossed about so violently that the compass was almost useless, it was entirely different!

On one tack the jib sheet parted so I seized the other one but it flapped madly and the whole ship shook. Dad managed to scramble forward and get the sail down before hoisting the reefed staysail.

As we beat up to the Ornsay harbour (formed between the island and the mainland) there seemed to be two ships at anchor. Once abeam of the windward one I luffed up while Dad pulled down the staysail and let go the anchor. He let out lots of chain, but it didn't seem to be holding and we were soon drifting rapidly to leeward. It was pitch dark but he managed to let go the kedge, which luckily was still on deck, and by the time he'd bent on another 50 fathoms of line she seemed to stop. While Dad was struggling with anchors and warps I managed to get the mainsail down and stowed. Since we seemed to be holding, there was nothing more we could do – although the shore seemed horribly close.

After cleaning up on deck we retired below to put on dry clothes and drink some hot soup. Dad had cut his finger and I'd cut my leg so we left blood stains on the sails and the cabin, but that probably sounds worse than it was; they were only superficial. As we relaxed and the tension eased we looked at each other and burst into laughter. After all, we go sailing for fun!

I'll never forget those three or four hours of blinding rain and spray as we careered from side to side of the Sound, wondering if the sails would split, the mast break, or whether *Emanuel* would smash herself to pieces on the rocks. Oh the relief of a quiet harbour.

We learnt later that the family had also spent a sleepless night, worrying that the caravan might be blown over in the high winds. Friends in Mull thought that the Oban ferry might even be cancelled. The wind was certainly stronger than it had been in the gale we experienced off the Sunk Light Vessel. Anyhow, the bad weather passed as quickly as it came and next morning the sun was shining and we had a light south-westerly breeze.

We weighed anchor and, having set the topsail and big jib, enjoyed a pleasant trip down the coast and round Ardnamurchan to Tobermory. According to one old sailing book, 'small boats have been known to drift for days trying to round Ardnamurchan'; luckily for us there was plenty of wind.

We went on a shopping expedition in Tobermory then then spent the next few days sailing with friends in Mull, calling in at Loch Aline and Oban. By September 5th we were off southwards again. We spent one night in Loch Don, where the milk for our breakfast came straight from the cows which lived in a field about two miles away. Pity the poor farmer's daughter who had to make the four mile round trip before we could have a cup of tea!

The winds were so variable that at one stage, as *Emanuel* passed close to some rocks, we almost needed the sweep! Finally, after accepting a tow from a passing fisherman, we anchored off Larne. From there to Helford (303 miles) we had a quiet and uneventful passage, though *Emanuel* seemed to be slower than usual. The reason was a thick growth of weed on her bottom which we discovered when we scrubbed and painted her at Helford.

Then it was on to the Yealm for the night; with no wind in the entrance, a couple of rowing boats gave us a tow. As we entered the river we passed a large flock of gannets feeding off a shoal of pilchards. What a super sight these handsome birds make, plunging down on their prey.

Then, off Bolt Head, on the last lap home, we saw a large four-masted Barque under full sail about three miles off. She looked so impressive; and to think that only few years earlier ships like her would have been commonplace!

The wind freshened from the south-west as we neared Anvil Point so we had to reef. Then we needed to gybe, but as the boom came over something went wrong, and the sail started unrolling over the dinghy. Dad went forward to investigate and found the pawl on the reefing gear had broken. He'd half expected it to happen for some time and had worked out a solution in his head. Relishing the chance to put theory into practice he lashed it up and everything was fine. We rounded Anvil Point safely and a couple of hours later were safely on our mooring at Lake above Poole.

Except for the tiny gap between Poole and Beaulieu, we'd sailed all the way round the coast of Great Britain – a distance of 1615 miles. It took us from July 30th to September 18th.

Track of *Emanuel* around Great Britain 1933

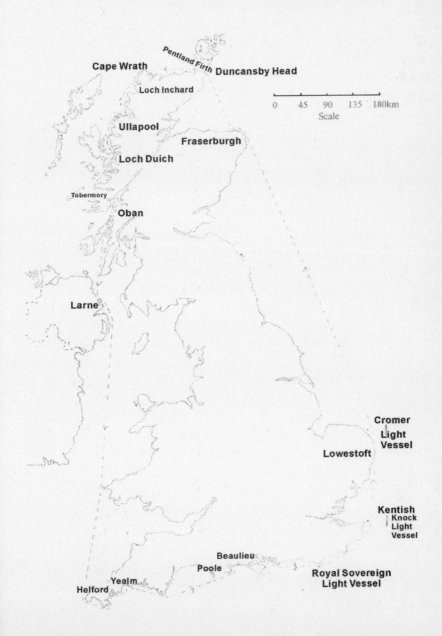

Cape Wrath

Pentland Firth

Duncansby Head

Loch Inchard

Ullapool

Fraserburgh

Loch Duich

Tobermory

Oban

Larne

Scale
0   45   90   135   180km

Cromer
Light
Vessel

Lowestoft

Kentish
Knock
Light
Vessel

Beaulieu

Poole

Royal Sovereign
Light Vessel

Yealm

Helford

Chapter Ten

FUN AND FAMILY IN ANTIGUA

As you can imagine, lying alongside the family villa at Jolly Bay was most relaxing.

The marina had excellent facilities with shops, restaurants and a pool – and a nearby beach where we spent a lot of time swimming. One day we sailed around to Deep Bay which was home to a tourist 'pirate ship' from which echoed much laughter and splashing. Two of the grandchildren managed to persuade Edward to let them have a go on a couple of jet bike machines, and I must say it looked fun. Had I been fifty years younger and more agile I would have joined in.

But I suppose age has its consolations; when visiting Nelson's Dockyard for a big party, I was delighted to find that they accepted my Hampshire Disabled Sticker.

The car park was quite a walk away, but they waived me through and let us drive right up to the entrance.

Antigua struck us as an island of contrasts – although parts have been developed for tourists, in other areas there's a sense of decay with fields unplanted and gaunt looking ruins of deserted sugar mills. The roads were a bit dicey too, though the wildlife was always interesting and in some of the more derelict open spaces we spotted large flocks of egrets.

After several days, on January 4th, the families returned home to jobs and schools, so *Mary Helen* and *Independent Freedom* moved on to St Martin.

The wind was a helpful Force 3, from the south which subsequently backed south-east before veering south-west and falling light just after dawn.

During the night, we picked up the lights of Nevis, St Christopher, St Eustatius, Saba and St Barthélemy, then anchored off Simpson Lagoon before the bridge opened at 1730. Finally, we made our way to the marina where I was astonished by the reception; the staff were incredibly warm and friendly – and had heard all about me. With *Independent Freedom* in the berth next to us I felt extremely happy and relaxed.

For the next fortnight, *Mary Helen* and *Independent Freedom* enjoyed some super, and at times boisterous sailing around St Martin – spending time in Grand Case, Tintamarre Island, Friars Bay and finally back to Marigot Bay.

The island itself, half of which belongs to Holland and half to France was busy and bustling and, apparently, the shared ownership works perfectly. Apart from the fact that the two countries spell the name differently, one would never know it was divided.

One of the highlights was Simpson Bay Marina where we caused quite a stir. Our small wooden ship stood out in sharp contrast to all the large plastic cruisers and we had numerous admirers. However, there was more to come, though I had no idea at the time. On Wednesday, January 10th 2001, one of the motoryacht owners arranged a surprise 89th birthday party for me. The chocolate cake was the biggest I'd ever seen! It was so kind and thoughtful – and, as I say, completely unexpected. It was also a chance to wear a startlingly bright outfit I'd bought in Antigua. I lost count of the number of drinks I consumed but was brought safely back on board in a motor buggy. But perhaps the ultimate gift came from the marina authorities who waived all their charges. Much appreciated!

Even the press turned up to interview me; the *Daily Telegraph* sent along a photographer as well as a reporter but the poor chap missed a flight along the way and eventually arrived only to discover that *Mary Helen* had already left. Fortunately he managed to get a message to us and was finally ferried out to our anchorage a little further along the coast.

Both he and the reporter were good fun. Not only that, they took us ashore for dinner and produced a really first-rate feature.

All in all then, this particular part of the adventure was particularly pleasurable. Hospitality apart, I shall always remember beating up the Anguilla channel and running down the eastern side – it was simply exhilarating.

When we left Marigot Bay on Wednesday, January 24th, for Anguilla, we were well reefed down. In the strong north-easterly wind *Mary Helen* was in her element – literally as well as metaphorically – cracking ahead like a racehorse at 6½ knots.

Even after rounding Anguillita Island on the south-western end of Anguilla, and hard on the wind, she continued slicing along much as before. The water was fairly flat, which obviously helped, but her performance was still impressive – so much so that we finally caught up with *Independent Freedom* in Road Bay and dropped our anchor just after she did.

Anguilla is a complete contrast to the lush, undulating and vibrant St Martin. Flat, scrubby and sleepy, it could hardly be more different. In many ways, of course, that's what makes this kind of cruising so stimulating. You never know what's coming next. The island is relatively unspoiled and though we found a small town with moderate shops, the whole place exudes a relaxed, almost lackadaisical atmosphere. There was supposed to be a race for cruising boats like ours, but in the end only locals took part. They manhandled their boats into the water, raced them precariously in a fresh breeze under full sail, then hauled them up again. It was hugely exciting.

One of the positive advantages of a place like this though was the absence of irritating jet skis. Such a relief!

On Friday January 25th Ian joined us and we went for a sail. It was a hot sunny day with light winds and a moderately large swell. Venturing out around Seal Island Reef, we saw some really large breakers which clearly indicated one of the obvious danger spots – then pushed on past Prickly Cays before returning back to Road Bay again.

Having got a taste of what might be described as the local attractions, we could well understand why the passage to Anegada has an infamous reputation in bad weather. With the wind blowing so hard, we were in no mood to test the validity of such reports at close quarters so prudently decided to remain where we were. It would be ten days before we finally left.

In the interim, we hired a car and went exploring. We also used the time to finish off a number of minor repairs and modifications.

At times, the anchorage was uncomfortable. Big, powerful swells surged in periodically which rolled us about violently – and most days saw rain in the squalls. To balance things up though, we were treated to some truly spectacular rainbows.

At last, on Monday February 5th the forecast promised something more conducive so that afternoon, in a south-easterly Force 3 – 4 *Mary Helen* cautiously set off.

To begin with, all went well and by nightfall, with the moon shining brightly, our little ship, rolling in the swell, was charging along with the wind astern. It was too good to last. Just before midnight we were struck by a heavy squall and torrential rain. The wind began to shriek its way up the Beaufort Scale until it reached a strident Force 8.

Approaching the Barracuda Bank we ran into nasty short seas which remained with us until we passed through Round

Island Passage and out into the grandly named Sir Francis Drake Channel. From there, we had a super sail right up to the Virgin Gorda Yacht Harbour.

After a night's rest we left for Anegada.

The weather was marvellous; warm and sunny with a spanking breeze. Not surprisingly, *Mary Helen* skated along through the crystal clear water.

After two days there, we enjoyed a fast, rough sail to Gorda Sound where we anchored off Prickly Pear Island. Three days on, we moved to Biras Creek and spent another few days anchored in a sheltered spot waiting for the wind to ease before making our way down to The Baths – an intriguing formation of rounded rocks with deep pools between.

The only drawback here was the anchorage which was rather open. In the evening we had supper aboard *Independent Freedom* and played Scrabble. But when it was time to return to *Mary Helen*, a mere hundred yards or so away, the boys flatly refused to let me climb into the dinghy which was bobbing about in the swell. I have to say I was rather indignant because I had no qualms about it at all. After some debate, however, I gave in graciously, with a smile, and spent the night on board.

The following day, with everything back to normal, we set off in *Mary Helen* and sailed to Marina Cay. The place was packed with charter boats – so much so that you felt they somehow contaminated the place. I also missed the old fashioned sense of camaraderie; once upon a time if you met other yachts in far away places you'd call on them or they'd call on you – but times have sadly changed!

From there, we went to Beef Island before making our way via Road Town, to Nanny Cay, Tortola. After two nights there, we continued to Diamond Cay at the north-eastern end of Jost Van Dyke Island. The passage across was brisk because of a passing squall but *Mary Helen* took it all in her stride. The next stop was Diamond Cay – after passing Sandy Cay – where we anchored on what eventually became a lee shore when the wind came round to the south-east. I'd never seen so many pelicans in one place; many seemed to be nesting in the mangrove trees and diving into the water. I didn't care to swim on such occasions in case one of them mistook me for a fish!

But, to be honest, there was little time for nature notes. As evening drew on, we became increasingly concerned about our safety.

It was an anxious night – not simply due to the wind direction but also because of the nearby reef. Next morning we were pleased to take our leave and ambled gently on to Great Bay just 3½ miles away.

We spent four nights there, then left for Cruz Bay, a small, crowded wash-ridden place, then got clearance into the American Virgin Islands and motored round to Fish Bay before anchoring near *Independent Freedom*.

Next day we sailed to Coral Harbour and back, then, on Wednesday, February 28th, set sail for Charlotte Amalie, St Thomas. It was a fine sunny day and we sauntered along between Great St James Island and Little St James Island. The passage was extremely narrow with the added attraction of a reef that meant we had to steer a dog leg course to clear it.

Having arrived, we made our way to the Ramada Marina which lies close to the cruise liner terminal. Three huge ships lying alongside dominated the view and dwarfed everything else in sight – which for us, made it all feel somewhat commercial – so, after taking on food and water, we left the following day.

As we passed the town through Haulover Cut and down the west side of the island to Flamingo Bay, the heavens opened and it poured with rain. This was a good place to anchor as long as you ignored the stream of locals whizzing by in fast, noisy motorboats on their way to the lagoon.

Flamingo was once a holiday resort but it was clear that a hurricane had swept through at some point and smashed the place to pieces. Now, little remained and nothing had been done to repair the damage.

After only one night we left early for Isla de Culebra. There was little wind until we got abeam of Saba Island where we passed the remains of a wrecked yacht. I suppose such things are akin to traffic accidents. You look, you reflect and move on.

In our case, we gently accelerated as the wind picked up, and made a fast passage past Sail Rock to Culebra where we anchored behind a protective reef which encircles Ensenada Honda. The water was calm and the breeze kept us cool.

Next day, we beat out of the narrow entrance between the reefs before bearing away and sailing past the southern end of Culebra towards Isla Palominos. It was incredibly pleasant – warm and sunny with a reasonably fair wind.

On arrival, we managed to pick up a buoy laid over a coral reef on the west side of the island. Strangely, for once, the natives were far from friendly and refused to let us land. Since this was merely an overnight stop, it was of little consequence but I was personally disappointed by the way the locals reacted.

Anyhow, we were soon on our way, leaving just after dawn. The day began sunny but later, as we cruised along the coast to San Juan, it clouded over. With a cracking, easterly wind, which steadily increased, we made good time. For a finale, a whale leapt clear of the water, and crashed back again, some 200 yards away.

We completed an exciting gybe and rounded up past the impressive old fort. For those who closed the coast in days of yore, this must have been an awesome sight.

Theatricalities over, we made fast in the Club Nautico Marina not far from *Independent Freedom*.

We spent five days in San Juan during which time we got busy with the varnish brush before stowing our provisions.

However, we did allow ourselves one day off during our stay and took a trip through the inland forest on the hill – then finally left on Saturday, March 10th bound for the Turks and Caicos Islands.

▲ *Mary Helen*, as good as new after her refit in Dartmouth, 1999.

▲ Ready for the off: Michael, Donald and me in *Mary Helen's* saloon.

The sturdy
saloon table
folds out and
can also be
used for chart
work.

A tribute to Christopher Columbus:
flag dancing in Madeira.

Leaving
Gomera with
a fair wind
astern.

▲ Ships that pass. This bulk carrier was particularly friendly, and wished us good luck.

▲ Donald's temporary lash-up after the goose-neck came adrift.

▲ The family at Nelson's Dockyard, Antigua. From left to right: John, Teddy, Donald, Emily, me, Camilla, Olivia, Edward and Ian.

◄ Hounded by the press? These chaps from the *Daily Telegraph* were absolutely charming.

Happy birthday to me. Everyone was so kind – and, as you can see, I made the most of it!

▼

Lights in the
sky at Road Bay.
How's that for
a rainbow?

Round-the-
world yachtsman
Ian completes
his three year
circumnavigation
in *Independent
Freedom*.

▲ The two of us: *Independent Freedom* and *Mary Helen* at anchor.

▲ Family fun. In *Mary Helen's* cockpit. From left to right: Marguerite, Ian, me, Teddy, Donald, Malcolm and Bids.

◀ Hardly gourmet food, but what we had was always nourishing. In this shot I'm still sporting bruises from my fall.

James (left) and Donald (above), beginning to take it easy as we enter the English Channel. I couldn't have done it without them.

James catching up with some much needed sleep. With the lee cloths in place, *Mary Helen's* bunks are surprisingly snug.

Home at last –
sailing into
Dartmouth.

The end of a great adventure.

Mother and son, back on the
Beaulieu River, surprised by
all the attention.

Mission accomplished.

We opted to take a route which left the Silver and Mouchoir Banks to windward, while *Independent Freedom* went inside. The winds varied enormously but we still managed a fast passage to Cockburn Harbour, South Caicos, arriving on Tuesday, March 13th.

After the necessary formalities, we sailed on to Six Hills Cays on the Caicos Bank. That meant heading out to sea again before cutting back across the reef – and keeping a careful lookout for coral heads. We anchored close to the Cays, and with the wind a feisty Force 5 from the east, spent an uncomfortable night before rising at dawn.

After an early breakfast, we promptly got underway and shaped a course for French Cay some 33 miles over the Caicos Bank. With a fresh easterly breeze, we quickly crossed the stretch of clear, turquoise water in company with *Independent Freedom* – but, as before, we found ourselves constantly watching the water for the slightest sign of coral.

After dropping the anchor we went ashore to take a look at four wrecks. I suppose they could have been Haitian fishing boats whose owners hoped for sanctuary in a British colony. By evening, it was blowing hard with short spikey seas. As a consequence our night was far from peaceful.

That was our cue to leave, and we set off for Sapodilla Bay, Providenciales, which meant crossing the Caicos Bank again. Under double-reefed main and staysail, we thundered across. The water was a delicate shade of blue through which we watched the white, sandy bottom – never more than a foot or two beneath *Mary Helen*'s keel – sliding effortlessly past.

The anchorage in Sapodilla Bay was particularly lumpy, especially with the wind blowing in as it was so we went ashore to make our final arrangements then left the following day.

Chapter Eleven

DON'T HIT THE CORAL HEADS

For our passage to the Bahamas we set our Atlantic rig which meant booming out the headsails – and in no time, as we left the Caicos Bank astern, were creaming through the darker, deeper waters of the Caicos Passage.

We wanted to visit San Salvador but the forecast warned of a deep front which would apparently pass by on the Tuesday or Wednesday. It seemed prudent therefore to head for Great Exhuma Island instead and look for shelter.

What followed was a mixed bag of conditions, from frustrating zephyrs to something more respectable – which took us through the Mayaguana Passage to the south of Samana and Rum Cay before we rounded the north end of Long Island and sailed westward towards Great Exhuma Island. At dawn, on Monday, March 19th, we sighted *Independent Freedom* hove-to.

Her route through the Mira Por Vos passage – which signified the end of her global circumnavigation – had been more westerly – but now she could join us as we made our way to Georgetown. Ian had taken just three years to get round which was quite an achievement. Having dealt with clearance we found a sheltered anchorage at Redshank Cays where we went ashore and celebrated the end of Ian's great adventure in a smart café at the water's edge.

After that, it was a case of riding out the front. For two nights we experienced thunder, lightning and torrential rain, but the days were absolutely fine! It gave me time to reflect.

I'm fascinated by islands. I suppose it all started when, at the age of 17, I made a trip with my father to the Færoes. I was so excited by the adventure that I kept a written record of it. My breathless account started like a ripping yarn: "During the evening of August 1st 1929 a little white yacht called *Emanuel*, named after a Bridgewater ship which sailed with Frobisher in 1518 to discover the North-West passages, passed through Bridgewater dock gates into the muddy waters of the River Parret".

As I explained in my essay, we had a young Oxford undergraduate with us as crew and the weather was fine. In fact, it was a beautiful evening but with little or no wind so with no engine we were stuck. Luckily, there was help at hand and a group of boys on the river bank towed us a short distance, before the tide took us a little further. However, about half a mile beyond the dock gates *Emanuel* grounded on the mud. We tried to get her off with the kedge but failed so gave up, had supper and turned in.

Next morning we got under way at about 0500, but grounded again a mile or two further on. In the afternoon we floated off, and at last cleared the bar. There was a breeze blowing and a slight chop in the channel – enough to make the motion fairly lively.

I was resting as we drew out of Burnham, and when I came on deck found the Crew looking green and unhappy. Since this was his first time at sea on a small boat it was hardly surprising. The skipper wasn't looking too brilliant, either, and asked me to go and get some biscuits from the foc'sle. I took a while because I stopped to mop up some paraffin which had spilt down below – and when I returned I felt slightly queasy as well. Both the Crew and the Skipper had been feeding the fishes, and I soon followed their example – an auspicious beginning!

Looking back, it was really rather funny, although it didn't seem that way at the time. Hush! "Tell it not in Gaoth, publish it not in the streets of Askelon," but I'd never seen the Skipper seasick before; honestly, he was worse than me!

Perhaps seasickness affects older people more; I certainly fared better than either of my two companions, and even took a spell at the helm. In the meantime, the Skipper retired below, as did the Crew, who decided to stretch out on my bunk (the most comfortable).

We reached Minehead at about 2200, and anchored under Greenalay point. Some five years earlier I'd tried to make a sketch of it, and as far as I remember, was moderately pleased with the result. Some time later I chanced upon a piece of paper, covered with weird blobs of paint. It was obviously meant to be a painting of sorts, but what? Suddenly it dawned on me. It was my sketch of Greenalay Point. I blushed and tore it up!

The Skipper was up early the following morning, and got under way singlehanded.

I joined him later, and we had breakfast together. There was enough wind for a reef in the mainsail but the sun was shining, and we had a glorious sail to Ilfracombe. Neither of us repeated the previous day's performance though the Crew only appeared after we'd anchored in the outer harbour at about 1015. We stowed the sails, and made everything ship-shape, then set off in search of our first substantial meal for 36 hours. After that, having more or less recovered, the Crew and I went ashore to shop, and left the Skipper with the washing up! Later we accepted a tow into the inner harbour, and made fast alongside the quay. After supper a friend of the Skipper's came on board, and we had a very pleasant evening.

There was talk of leaving early on Sunday morning, but the weather looked so bad that we decided to wait. Eventually we left Ilfracombe at 1630, and had a fine sail across the Channel. It was the first time the Crew had felt OK.

We approached the Welsh shore as it was getting dark, and, as I recall, it seemed to me that we were very close to the rocks. The breakers roared angrily, and at one point I could have sworn I saw a line of foam, though I may have imagined it.

At last we anchored in Oxwich Bay, in the early hours of the morning, and turned in for a few hours of sleep. Skipper and Crew were up early, and I joined them for breakfast. There was a slight sea, and the Crew had to eat his egg on deck. After breakfast both men turned in, and I sailed *Emanuel* towards Caldy.

When we drew close to the island, the Skipper came on deck, and we anchored in Caldy Road around about noon. We stretched our legs on the island, and then returned. The weather was less than promising, but we sailed up to the entrance of the Sound to check things out. The Skipper's log was blunt, 'N.B.G.'. My diary notes, 'Not worth going out,' were milder but the meaning was the same. We returned to Tenby, berthed alongside the jetty, then walked into town and went to the cinema.

The following morning, Skipper and Crew got underway early. I was up at about 0600. I should remark, at this point, that a naval officer's log is supposed to be an accurate account, but on this occasion however, the Skipper wrote, 'Smell of breakfast induced Mate to turn out'. This was far from the truth. My real motive in fact was a sudden feeling that unless I went up on deck *ad statim* I'd be seasick. However, I managed to eat some breakfast, and was soon perfectly all right again.

After rounding St Govern's, we found we could steer a course up the Irish Sea.

The conditions for making a passage were good, so our original idea of putting into Milford Haven was abandoned – and with the Crew fast asleep below, we decided to continue. Skokham and Skomar were visible up ahead, and after giving me the precise course to steer, the Skipper went below for a rest.

I told the Crew about our changes in plans. He seemed a bit surprised, but said nothing. Later on though, when Skoma was abeam and the Skipper came up, he asked to be put ashore at Fishguard. I nearly fell overboard with surprise. Apparently he couldn't cope with the seasickness.

Well, *Emanuel* had nearly stood on her head when we passed through St Govern's race that morning so perhaps it wasn't surprising.

The Skipper went below to look at the charts, etc, and discovered that the glass had suddenly dropped. Accordingly we decided to go into Ramsey Sound, and land the Crew at St David's Head. We eventually anchored in a little bay, where we saw two French fishing boats. We went across to them and asked if they could supply us with something for supper. Not only did they give us some fish – we also came back with a rabbit! Skipper was very pleased with himself, because he knew what 'un lapin' was. Our offer of money was swept aside so we gave them some beer. They were most appreciative and said they'd noticed me at the helm when we came in. While they were talking, I caught the words 'matelot' and 'soldat' and hoped the latter referred to my father rather than to me! They also kindly agreed to land the Crew the following morning.

The Skipper and I went for a row before breakfast. We tried to land but the cliffs were too steep to climb. On the other hand, as I said at the time, had we been pursued by a horde of savages I think we might have managed it! The shore itself was very weather beaten and eaten away. At one point we found we could row right into a cave where the waves thundered in such an alarming and threatening manner we were glad to get out; it was marvellous to see the sunlight again. After breakfast we landed at a proper jetty and walked around the island. We had a glorious view from the top and spotted Grassholm, the Smalls, and Bishop in the distance. After lunch the fishermen called for the Crew and he left.

We left Ramsay around 1700, and in a light, northerly breeze we reached Fishguard by the evening and anchored for the night. Early the following morning, on August 8th we left. To start with there was hardly any wind, so we the made the most of it by taking some snaps of *Emanuel*. There's something thrilling about a ship under sail, and with the sunlight gleaming on her shimmering white sails, *Emanuel* looked fantastic. After lunch, we picked up a westerly breeze, and were soon racing along at six knots, heading north, up the Irish Sea. At last we were getting somewhere. The previous week had been a really hard slog.

I turned out at about 0300 and in the dim distance, picked out the Mourne Mountains and Slieve Donnard, showing faintly against the pink sky of dawn. The breeze held till we reached the South Rock Light Vessel at dusk, when it fell away, and left us rolling in the swell. The damp mist, which enveloped us, soon developed into rain which, along with a thick fog stayed with us for most of the night; the sea remained oily smooth. Early the following morning we crawled along in light airs to Donaghadee, where we anchored. Most of the day was spent cleaning up on board. Then some friends from Belfast turned up for tea and afterwards took us for a drive. There was talk of going on in the evening, but the weather was wet, and we were feeling very tired; well, anyway I was. During supper I could only just keep my eyes open!

Next day we left Donaghadee, still heading north. It was most exciting spotting the Mull of Cantyre and Ailsa Craig – our first glimpses of Scotland. The morning after, we sailed through Islay Sound, passing some tiny and fascinating-looking islands called 'Isles of the Sea'. They were jagged, and scarred by the waves, while surf, breaking on the rocks, formed a protective ring of white, in sharp contrast to the deep blue sea beyond.

We sailed into the entrance of Mull Sound. The scenery was wonderful, and so different from the 'green hills o' Somerset' to which we were accustomed. We anchored in Loch Don and went ashore for milk which came straight from the cow. We enjoyed a lovely view over the Lochs. The mountain tops were clad in bright purple heather, which softened on the way down, until it met the vivid blue of the water below. Later in the evening we beat up to Ardtonish Bay, anchored, had supper and turned in.

Next morning we sailed through the Sound of Mull, and headed for the western extremity of Skye, spending the night at sea. When I turned out, about 0230, it began to rain. It's a curious fact that it always rains on my watch. Anyway, it was teaming down and for once I wasn't keeping a very good lookout. Part of the problem was the fact that unless you stood up, the dinghy blocked the view to starboard. Suddenly I heard a swishing of water, and a little drifter shot across our bows. They yelled a cheery "good morning", and continued on their way. What a shock! I thought we'd hit a reef, or something.

As we neared Stornaway we saw swarms of drifters entering the harbour. We entered on a beat in a light airs, which soon deserted us so we had to sweep the yacht across the harbour, right through the stream of fishing boats. I'm sure some of them were annoyed and they made us roll in their wakes. We had tea ashore, and later on saw a Man-of-War anchor; we also watched the arrival of the mail boat, the great event of the day at Stornaway. This time she bought with her crowds of fisher girls, who came for the herrings. Some fishermen said we were mad to think of going to the Færoes!

August 15th was the first day we stopped sailing. We spent the morning shopping, and in the afternoon called on H.M.S. *Rosemary* for a chronometer comparison. In reality it was an excuse for the Skipper to go aboard a Man-of-War again. We were very well received, and stayed to tea and dinner. Next morning we had lunch in the *Rosemary* then took their pilot, Lieut. H.L. Jenkins for a sail to Loch Erisfort. It was delightful, and the view across Loch Erisfort was stunning. Saturday's weather was too bad for sailing but H.M.S. *Flinders*, which had just come in, invited us on board, so off we went.

Sunday, August 18th, saw us bound for the Færoes at last. We left after breakfast in brilliant sunshine and sailed north. Eventually I saw the murky shape of the Butt beyond the coastline.

"Shall we go on?" asked the Skipper.

"Rather," I replied.

We made excellent progress, and by the Tuesday morning were ready to make a landfall.

It was extremely foggy with a vile irregular swell and no wind. Skipper's sights failed to tally with his dead reckoning position, so we decided to take some soundings. After joining all the thin line we had on board, and arming the lead with grease, we lowered it over the side, struck the bottom at sixty fathoms, and brought up a piece of shell. It was only in the afternoon that we sighted land, and even then it was to port, instead of starboard. As we drew near, we gradually made out the entrance to Trangisvaag.

The coastline was high and mountainous with a magnificent cliff at the entrance of the fjord, which rose out of the sea until it disappeared in the clouds hanging over the hills. As we sailed up the fjord we were struck by the quaint, foreign appearance of the houses. There were also some curious Beehive shaped lumps here and there along the shore. As we later discovered they were mounds of partially dried fish.

No sooner had we anchored than several boatloads of people turned up to look at us. We seemed to puzzle them greatly. Then the harbour master came on board, and took our names etc, for the local newspaper. Since we were tired after our 214-mile passage from Stornaway, we stayed on board, had supper, and turned in.

Next morning, before breakfast, we were hailed, and a man in a boat who presented us with a 'Memento of Færoe' a local sketch in oils, which he'd painted himself. It was a charming picture, and was given place of honour in *Emanuel's* cabin. Our visitors name was Sigmund Petersen.

In my diary I made the following remarks: 'This morning, so far (1100) nine boats have been out to see us, mostly manned by small boys, but one with a party of girls. Apparently the boys are allowed to come by themselves, but the girls have to be accompanied.

We went ashore around noon, and were greeted on the jetty, by crowds of small children, who gazed at us with such rapt attention that we felt a little embarrassed. Gradually though, we got used to it.

A fisherman told one of the boys to take us to the Custom's Office, and the larger and bolder boys led the way, the rest following behind. It was quite a royal procession! The Harbour Master, Mr Hanson, was most amiable, and directed us to the hotel, where we ordered lunch.

The soup was thick with grease and was brought in at the same time as the meat which looked like lumps of mud and was cold by the time we were ready to eat it. It was boiled mutton from from Little Dimon, a small precipitous island which evidently encouraged strong, sturdy animals.

The landlady thought that one Krone each (about 10p) was too much, but we persuaded her to take it, so she insisted on making me a pair of traditional sheepskin shoes. Everyone wore them. The girls had red strings attached, while the boys had white. Some of the men wore heavier cow's hide shoes; they also wore national dress, which consists of breeches, tight about the knees, fastened by a number of silver buttons, and a loose, natural brown coat with more buttons down the front. Their stockings and coats were usually home spun and woven. Their hats, curiously-shaped caps, were striped, either white and blue, or red, white, and blue. The girls wore modern clothes. Their language comes from an old Norse dialect, and at that time had only recently been written down.

Old Mr and Mrs Petersen were unable to write Færoeese, but, of course, they could speak it. They were also able to write in Danish, the official language. At school they learnt Danish, Færoeese and English. Nearly everyone spoke a little English, which they picked up chiefly from trawlers that stopped on their way to Iceland. We had no difficulty in making ourselves understood.

After lunch we walked out to the end of the fjord, which offered magnificent views. There were telegraph wires all along the road, which, in effect was just a glorified path, and quite impossible to wheeled traffic.

We saw a number of men in national dress with short, straight-bladed scythes, cutting tiny patches of hay which grew wherever the land permitted it. We also passed a few minute patches of corn.

Their cows were kept tethered to the wayside and must have lived sad, lonely lives. Had they been free to roam however, they would probably have fallen over the cliff.

What struck us above all, was the contrast between old and new. There were electric lights and telegraph poles along the road, yet, apart from the odd bicycle all you saw were people on foot. Similarly, whereas the old men wore national dress the girls showed off their silk stockings and fur-necked coats. Inside the cottages you might see a woman spinning, with a telephone at her elbow.

On the way back to the boat, we met Mr Petersen, who invited us to his home. We were unsure whether he meant for supper or not. I thought he said something about food, but the Skipper was less certain. We were starving after our walk, but decided to eat only a light meal in case we had a meal at the Petersen's later. Thankfully, I'd heard right. Their food was infinitely better than the hotel's. I was confused though; were we meant to use the same plate all the time? Apparently we were.

Old Mr and Mrs Petersen were charming and had such extraordinarily kind faces. The gathering included three cousins, Sigmund, Lula and Joanna.

The two girls had their meals in the kitchen, and joined the rest afterwards. Sigmund and Mr Petersen could speak quite good English, Mrs Petersen just a little, and the others none. We were just about to go, at about 2130, when they gave us some delicious pineapple and cream. Afterwards, the younger members of the family accompanied us back to *Emanuel* where we gave them some beer. They were very taken with the boat.

After breakfast the following day, Sigmund came over and asked if we would take him with us to Thorshavn. The wind was extremely squally, so we only set the storm jib, reefed main, and staysail. Outside, the seas were steep and irregular. As a backdrop, we had those magnificent cliffs, straight and sheer, soaring to great heights against the darkening sky.

As we neared Thorshavn we passed a couple of tiny Viking boats. Anyway that's what they looked like. They were marvellous to watch, as, plunging heroically, they took the seas head on – rearing up on the crests, with half the boat out of the water, then crashing down again with a splash, without taking a drop of water on board. There was only one man in each boat, and each looked thoroughly relaxed. One knew Sigmund, and the two men exchanged cheerful greetings. It was most exhilarating.

We reached Thorshavn in the afternoon. It's the capital so much larger than Trangisvaag, and really more of a town. There were even a few cars there. We landed before a crowd of astonished children. One boy took us to the hotel. Having learnt English at school, he could speak it quite well and seemed glad to have an opportunity of making practical use of his knowledge. Sigmund gave us dinner.

I shall never forget it. We had liver, one of the few things I really don't like! There was some melon on the table something the Skipper really loved. Every now and then he glanced at it longingly, but it never came our way!

After dinner Sigmund took us for a walk around the town. One of the shops was displaying some of his pictures. They were exceedingly good. He taught himself to paint, but I felt sure he could have been famous had he studied at art school in Europe.

The following morning we called at the British Consulate, but the Consul was away on holiday so Sigmund took us to a house where they sold hand-made knitwear. After buying a jersey, we were invited to partake of tea and cake with the family.

We lunched at the sailors' home, which was considerably better than the hotel. One old man asked dozens of questions about *Emanuel* and her voyage. Each time we answered, his response was the same. "That's good," he replied. I think he could understand.

After lunch we were taken in a Chevrolet to Kirkebö. It was once the largest town in Færoe, until an avalanche pushed the houses into the sea. There was no loss of life because everyone sheltered in the church.

The drive was rather nerve-racking, for the road was stony and narrow. Periodically we encountered hairpin bends and right-angled turns. It was also extremely steep, with the deep fjord below ready and waiting for us should our driver lose a moment's concentration.

Down there, the high wind was lashing the apparently smooth water, several British trawlers were running into Thorshavn for shelter. We arrived at Kirkebö without mishap, and were shown the remains of an old church, which was never completed.

According to local legend, the Bishop who was building it fell out with the locals, who tried to kill him. He escaped to the top of the wall by means of a secret passage, and remained there for three days. However, the strain proved too much for him, and he fell off, and was torn to pieces by the mob.

The farmhouse was a fascinating place and built on a foundation of stone, which contained an ancient dungeon. The top was made of wooden logs, which they assured us were 900 years old. The living room was like a large, traditional English farmhouse – except for the greased whaling spears hung on one of the plain timber walls. In another corner was a stone quern. Down the middle of the room was a wooden table, with a couple of bare wooden benches.

Mr Patursen, the farm's owner, was one of the chief Færoemen and a representative in the Danish parliament, as well as leader of the Home Rule Party.

Above all though what made our visit to the village so pleasant was the simple fact that they treated us as guests, rather than tourists. Wherever we went, we were never allowed to leave without having something to eat and drink – usually tea and cakes. There was a large garden at Kirkebö, too, the largest in the Islands. Our guide offered us some of the delicious strawberries that grew there. The Skipper, having picked several tons of strawberries earlier in the season, was understandably blasé about it, and declined. However, we were pressed to try them, and, to my great relief, he relented. I was never blasé about strawberries.

I was also shown a spinning wheel and allowed to try my hand on it. It looked easy, but I was singularly unsuccessful.

We dined at the sailor's home, where we met three Englishmen who'd been fishing. They were going home by the mail boat that evening. Next morning, the 24th, we got underway at about 1100. We dipped our ensign to a Danish Man-of-War, which smartly answered our salute, then had a glorious sail to Klaksvig. The sun came out for the first part of our passage, and the cliffs made a wonderful sight at the entrance to Lervig Sound. Looking through the Sound, it resembled an avenue of enormous, purple pyramids, their colours thinning as they faded into the distance.

We had to beat through the Sound, and it soon started to blow, but the water was smooth, and I found it exhilarating struggling with the helm and sheets.

We gybed as we entered Klaksvig Fjord, at which point the mainsheet, which I was pulling with all my strength, took charge, and ran out, leaving a bright red line down my leg where it rubbed. Just as we anchored, it poured with rain, so we got absolutely drenched. Afterwards the cabin felt even more cosy than normal.

The next day was a Sunday so we went ashore for a walk. After climbing about 1000ft up a mountain, the Skipper was delighted to find some unusual plants apparently of Arctic origin. The hillside was boggy and wet with numerous waterfalls. I was bare-legged and more comfortable in my sandals than skipper was in his socks and boots, which got incredibly wet. On our return, at about 1630, we went to the 'Hotel British' and asked for tea. After the proprietress of the hotel had told us her family history, and mistaken me for a girl of 12 or 13 (I was, of course, 17 and once before had been referred to as the Skipper's wife) we were provided with a sort of high tea, with lots of dried meat which was rather strong. The old lady said she liked the English and had met a great number of sailors from British trawlers.

" I haf neveer meet one bad Engleeshman, so I call my place 'Hotel British," she explained.

It made us feel rather proud. She flatly refused to let us pay for our meal, and even gave us some milk as well. Where in England, I wondered, would that sort of thing happen? As we were walking back to the boat, the end of the Skipper's pipe fell off. As he turned to pick it up, his sudden movement frightened the following crowd of children who quickly ran away! However, when they realised what was happening, they thought it rather funny. The Skipper rashly said that anyone who wanted to could come on board. There was great excitement, and dozens of children descended on us. At one time there were so many on the stern that we started taking in water. Our first visitors had cake, but that soon ran out. In the end, seventy one people, of all ages and sex, came to look us over. Some of the boys came twice. It was rather an exhausting evening.

We left Klaksig at about 0830 the following day and had a delightful sail through Harald Fjord before anchoring near the Narrows in Kvanne Sund. We then went ashore and examined a derelict whaling station. There was little to be seen – just a few bones. We left Kvanne Sund in the afternoon and spent the evening becalmed near the entrance. The cliffs and hills were magnificent, and in the distance we could see Cape Myling, which looked about eight miles away but in fact was some sixteen miles off. We also saw Fuglo behind Videro, which meant we'd seen both the most northern and most western extremities of the

Islands. Gradually, with the help of occasional puffs of wind and the tide, we drifted past Kadlur Head, en route for Funding fjord, which we reached in the early hours of the morning.

Next day we were again becalmed off the mouth of the fjord, but later found enough wind to take us down to Cape Myling, where it died away completely. Cape Myling is a most impressive cliff. With rocky caves at its base, it rises from the sea to a height of nearly 2,000 feet.

We gradually made our way down to Vestmanna Sund, where we found a fresh, squally breeze that took us up to Vestmanhavn, where we anchored, had supper, and went to bed. We went ashore after breakfast the following morning, and bought some badly needed bread; we'd been living on ship's biscuits for the previous few days. We were unable to buy any butter though.

We then called on a trawler, the *St Endellion*, to ask for a chronometer comparison, our usual excuse. We were entertained in the captain's cabin, under the bridge, where there were several other trawler skippers. A girl seemed a bit out of place, but they made me feel at home. The ship was extraordinarily well fitted out and clean. The skipper, Captain MacGreggor, had been born in Russia but was a naturalised British subject. We had an enormous tea on board, after which Russian George, as he was nicknamed, told us thrilling stories about Russia before the war.

His brother had been sentenced to twenty years in Siberia, but, after ten years, was released at the onset of war. George himself had run away to sea. After serving in various Russian ships he came to the conclusion that British sailors had a better time and joined the British Merchant Service. He told us how one day some Cossacks had come into the schoolroom, and asked questions – flicking their whips on the desks which made cuts a quarter-of-an-inch deep.

The weather was too bad for sailing that evening, so we stayed in the harbour.

Mr Sam Olsen took us up to an inland lake the following morning. We had an exhilarating climb up. It was blowing hard, and raining, but the exercise kept us warm. When we arrived we had to wait about and watch Mr Olsen wading knee-deep in freezing water. That alone was enough to make anyone feel cold, but the wind and rain almost turned us into icicles. However, we managed to keep our circulation going by running silly races, which had no beginnings or ends. We only caught a single fish, because it was blowing so hard. We also saw some specimens of the Arctic hare among the rocks.

Mr Olsen gave us coffee and cakes when we returned; then we went on board again, and changed into dry clothes. Færoe jerseys are wonderful garments. I was wearing one, with no coat or mackintosh, yet in spite of continuous rain all morning, remained perfectly dry underneath it.

In the evening we went on board the *Islands Falk*, a Danish gunboat, to buy some butter but they refused our offer of payment. The officers were all very friendly, spoke very good English and gave us a weather report, as well as a news bulletin about trouble in Palestine.

We got under way the following morning, but were becalmed for most of the day. There were a number of small Færoe boats about catching Fulmars. They just motored up to them and fished them up in a net. Why the idiotic birds let them do it was beyond my comprehension. One boat came up to us, and offered us a bird – but we politely declined. The mass of quivering white feathers in the bottom was enough to put anyone off.

We then passed through the Troll's Finger – a fine needle-like rock. Sigmund had told us the legend surrounding it, but we never quite understood the story. I think it had something to do with a wicked witch who attacked sailors.

The breeze was so light that we decided to go into Sandvaag. As it grew dark the wind freshened, and when I came up on deck I was alarmed to find us so close to the shore, near a line of breakers. We went about, and crossed over to the opposite shore, which was also rather noisy so we turned and fled for Trangisvaag. By 0230 we were just off the entrance; at 0330 we anchored, and turned in.

After breakfast, at 0930 the Petersens came and invited us to lunch. We showed the old people over the ship, and they seemed particularly interested. Then we got under way and, accompanied by a large proportion of the population in boats, sailed down the fjord, dipping our ensign on the way to *Islands Falk*.

Outside, we had a strong breeze, and horrible rain. The glass started to fall sharply, and after a few hours the Skipper decided things weren't good enough for making a passage, so we turned back and re-anchored in Trangisvaag.

The next day, Sunday, September 1st, the Petersens took us fishing. It didn't rain at first, but of course later on it poured. There was a thick fog, and we could see nothing, but the Petersens seemed to know the way. The roads, or rather tracks, are marked by cairns and it would have been easy to get lost.

When we arrived at the lake one of the boys lent me a pair of waders; I was very grateful. They offered a pair to the Skipper who manfully refused, because one of them would have had to go without. We fished with worms and caught dozens. The Skipper caught the first one, but I caught the biggest! I caught four altogether. It was great fun, but rather cold and damp.

We climbed home, and after changing on board, returned to the Petersens for supper. They'd killed a chicken specially for us, because they realised that their dried meat and boiled mutton was not to our liking. Mr Petersen and one of the boys stayed behind to catch some more fish, but they missed their way, and got back very late. After supper they sang old Færoe folk songs some of which were charming, and most expressive.

We left Færöerne on the Monday. Sigmund and Thorolo came over in the morning with milk and cakes, along with our clothes, which had been kindly dried for us. A few days later, while putting on a clean blouse, I discovered a piece of paper in the pocket, signed "Thorolo" and bearing the words: "ei kán laik ju veni ves". No one has ever managed to translate it for me.

We again dipped our ensign to the *Islands Falk*, while *S.S. Emerald* hooted to us, so we replied with our little tin whistle of a foghorn.

The exit was spectacular. We were accompanied to the mouth of the fjord by a number of small rowing and motor boats then had a super sail outside, making six knots with a reefed mainsail. Gradually the Færoes receded into the distance, until eventually we lost sight of them completely. Adieu, Færoe! We'd had a jolly fortnight sailing among the 'little rock Islands of the Atlantic', as Sigmund so aptly described his home, and we were sorry to see the last of them.

After completing 74¼ miles in twelve hours the wind dropped and we spent most of Tuesday becalmed. In the morning we both turned in. At about 1100 we heard a siren. Getting up to investigate we found a trawler, which, we decided, had come to see what a yacht was doing with no one at the helm. Around 1700 a breeze arrived and took us to within sight of North Rona; but the effort was clearly too much for it, and it finally collapsed, leaving us to wallow, so we hoisted a riding light and turned in. Early the following morning the revitalised breeze took us to Stornaway, where we anchored at about 2215.

The next day we were under way at 0230, and finally reached South Rona. Then the wind left us, and we spent another night becalmed. However, by the following morning we had a decent breeze and enjoyed a delightful sail through Kyle Akin, the inner passage between Skye and the Mainland. We anchored for the night in Loch Beiste, a beautiful little loch where the woods reach right down to the water's edge. We were much impressed with the beauty of these Scottish lochs and highlands, but it's beyond my powers to describe them.

Next day, Saturday, September 7th, was very murky, and in spite of a light wind managed to get down the Sound of Sleat to Dun Bane, where we anchored for a tide. Sunday was a repetition of Saturday, with fog and head winds, but we still sailed as far as the Island of Eigg. Next morning we saw two yachts outside, so we got under way and tried to catch them up. We hoisted our topsail, and started closing the gap on one of them, a black yawl, but she hoisted her balloon foresail, and ran away from us. The other yacht, another yawl, stood further out. We cut off a corner rounding Ardnamurchan, and by the time we reached Oban she was a hull down behind us. We spent Tuesday in Oban, and on Wednesday got down to Scarba Island. We rounded Cantyre on Thursday evening.

On Friday the Skipper had a rotten cold, so we went into Peel, on the Isle of Man. Saturday was spent in harbour. We left Peel on Sunday, and spent the next few days with hardly any wind. By Tuesday afternoon we reached the Bishop, but were almost becalmed. When I turned out on Wednesday morning we were abeam of St Anne's Lighthouse with St Govern's Light Ship ahead. We then had a wonderful sail. It was thrilling speeding up the Channel under full canvas with a fair breeze, picking up the old familiar headlands as we went. As we neared Minehead the great question was, "Could we catch the tide into Burnham, and up to Bridgewater?" We rushed through the water, a frantic race against time, but we won! We caught the tide just in time to sail up the Parret,

We were understandably excited when we dropped anchor outside the dock gates, yet sorry that it would be another twelve months before *Emanuel* felt the 'wash and thresh of the sea foam'. She'd looked after us extremely well.

Track of *Emanuel* 1929 Færoe Islands

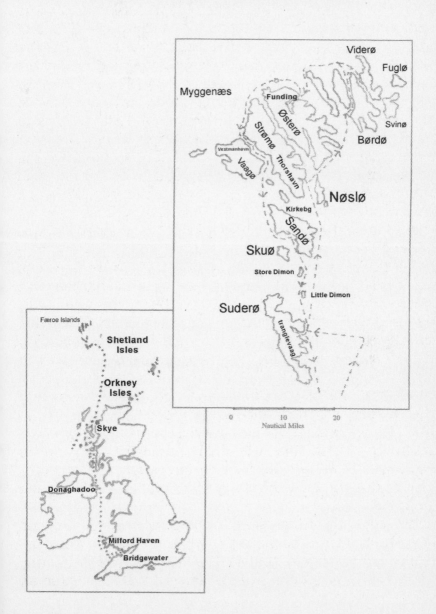

Chapter Twelve

BAHAMAS

Back in the Bahamas, it was time to go. We left on Friday, March 23rd – sailing past Georgetown and out through the northern entrance to Exhuma Sound – then headed north, fairly close to the reef, against a fairly light head wind which eventually blew from a slightly more helpful direction. Even so, *Mary Helen* was still finding conditions difficult so we motored through the night.

In the middle of Conch Cut, as we passed through and out on to the Great Bahama Bank, we encountered a powerful tide rip but *Mary Helen* never faltered. Incidentally, I was taken by the large number of other yachts about at the time. They were sailing both north and south so it felt really busy.

By late afternoon we were anchored off Allan Cay, a quiet, peaceful, spot. With no swell, no wind and just a gentle swell it was idyllic.

The next day we pressed on to New Providence Island which meant taking a dog leg to avoid the Yellow Bank and its dangerous coral heads. Since there was no wind, we had to start the engine. The water was as clear as gin, right down to the seabed.

Tucked away from the main channel and protected by an island, in theory at least, Nassau should have a lot going for it; in practice, I'm afraid, it's best avoided. The only decent marina was very expensive and, apparently, permanently full. We were directed to East Bay Marina a somewhat run down sort of place with a rickety, rusty pier in a far from salubrious part of the town. We had to pass under a large bridge to get there but Ian's mast was too tall so he had to find an anchorage outside where the continual passage of speeding motor boats whizzing past made life aboard most uncomfortable.

However it wasn't all gloom, some of the family would be coming out and there were good (expensive) shops near the cruise liners' berth. We were also lying alongside an American yacht and quickly made friends. The owner's wife even managed to find me an embroidery shop where I stocked up with thread.

Finally, the family arrived. My sister Marguerite came, so did Malcolm and his wife Bids, along with Donald's Lucy and their youngest son Teddy. They were booked into one of the 'tourist' complexes, which, compared to life on board, was comparative luxury.

Marguerite, three years younger than me, had been determined to fly out and come aboard *Mary Helen* though I'm not sure whether her doctor should have allowed it. On the other hand, Grahams are stubborn, and rarely take kindly to advice, so once her mind was made up, it probably wouldn't have made any difference. Unfortunately the long air journey made her ill, so she had to go back early. Malcolm's wife, Bids, had been a nurse and organised everything with meticulous efficiency while I spent a couple of nights in the hotel, keeping Marguerite company.

Later, the others found a Club Mediterrané. It sounded fun; having paid their entry fee they could eat and drink as much as they liked. Much to their delight, Donald and Teddy won a race in Hobie Cats beating Ian and his crew. When hiring the boats Donald was asked if he knew how to sail!

Once the families had gone home we set off again. Understandably, we were glad to leave the place behind, and chugged out in company with *Independent Freedom* on April 10th at 0600. Motoring towards the Berry Islands, the sea was glassy flat and the sky stayed clear all day. But having anchored off the southern end of Bird Island, suddenly, and as if to taunt us, a cool, steady breeze arrived – a perfect wind for sailing but, of course, several hours too late. Typical!

The following day we made our way to Chub Cay, inside the Diamond Rocks, where we hoped to find an anchorage for lunch. After a slow, leisurely sail in brilliant sunshine we anchored near the entrance to Chub Cay marina, which gave us a little more than a foot of water beneath the keel at low water.

On Thursday, April 12th, in an east-south-easterly Force 2 – 3 we pushed on towards Morgans Bluff on Andros Island. At 0950, we were nearly run down. We were crossing a wide stretch of calm water in perfect visibility and sailing peacefully along, close hauled, carefully watching a ship which had just left one of the islands.

It looked as though she'd have to alter course to miss us, but for some reason she kept ploughing on. I held a steady line as the Collision Regulations dictate, until at last I could bear it no longer and had to tack smartly to avoid a collision!

There seemed to be no one on the bridge, so Donald called him up on the radio. There was some delay before he answered, and when he did, Donald fairly let him have it and at one point questioned his parentage. Even Ian, who'd been astern of us had contacted them. I was furious too, because until then we'd been ahead of Ian and now we'd lost our lead! Donald sent a report to the Nassau authorities who they said they'd look into it.

Fortunately, the entrance to Morgans Bluff is well marked; unfortunately, it's difficult to pick out clearly until you get relatively close. It's also fairly hazardous with outlying reefs marked by thundering breakers. It was quite a relief to drop the anchor but our respite was short lived and we were plagued by persistent horseflies.

The next morning we rose early and said goodbye to Lucy and Teddy who left to catch their flight out. Then the two yachts weighed anchor, hoisted their sails and shaped a course back to the Berry Islands. With a generous beam wind and a gentle sea, progress was fast, and after some wonderful sailing, we dropped the hook at the northern end of Frozen Cay. Being in an excellent anchorage in settled weather was most comforting and we spent a peaceful night here before moving a mile northwards and anchoring in Little Harbour which, almost enclosed by Cays, is incredibly sheltered.

We stayed for a couple of nights before heading north again. To begin with, the wind was a westerly Force 2 but steadily increased and began to head us. Soon we were hard on the wind and making heavy weather of it, with *Mary Helen*'s bowsprit bucking, dipping and disappearing from time to time. It simply wasn't good enough. We needed to crack along much faster than this to get to Great Harbour Cay. It was time to make a decision. In the end we opted for Goat Cay which was not only a good deal closer but also offered shelter from the wind and promised to make an excellent anchorage.

Finally, nearing our destination, the wind died away, which the Bahamian air force seemed to think was a signal to dive-bomb us. Most exciting!

We left Goat Cay reasonably early in the morning in a light southerly wind, under a clear blue sky. Unfortunately, there's not enough water to head south from Goat Cay to Great Harbour Cay marina; which means heading out to sea, leaving Great Stirrup and Little Stirrup Cay to port before rounding the western end of Little Stirrup Cay and heading back south over the Great Bahama Bank. You then head south-east toward the Corinth-like cut. The passage completed, we motored into the marina and made fast alongside *Independent Freedom*.

The weather though warm, was far from kind. It blew hard from the north-east for six days – which gave us time to catch up with our chores. There was yet more varnish work, along with numerous other odd jobs to occupy our time. We also repaired the jib.

It was Tuesday, April 24th when we left Great Harbour Cay for West End at the western tip of Grand Bahama Island. The forecast was OK until Thursday when another front was due. We retraced our steps back over the Great Bahama Bank, before shaping a course of 320° for West End, leaving Little Stirrup Cay about two miles to starboard.

We started well enough, striding along in an east-south-easterly Force 3 breeze – then, just off the bank, ran into heavy seas and a powerful swell. Even in such modest conditions it was hardly a picnic; what the north-west providence channel would be like in really bad weather I could only imagine. There were many ocean liners about – but all of them were plodding along fairly slowly. After dark, clouds began to gather, the first slow movement in a natural sonata. The climax was explosive thunder and dazzling lightning which crackled into life just after dawn. The blackness was total; it enveloped us completely. There was little or no wind – just bangs and flashes – and rain. Visibility was almost zero, the decks were awash and fresh water from the cockpit started filling the bilges – which triggered the automatic bilge pump. All this continued for some time and only abated as we approached West End. We made fast in the marina at 1000 and received a much appreciated warm welcome from the staff; *Independent Freedom* was moored nearby.

We were weather bound in West End for a fortnight, as indeed were several other yachts. While we sheltered from the strong north-easterly wind one or two of the larger yachts got away but after weighing everything up Ian said he thought it best to wait, so stayed to keep us company.

We hired a car and went exploring. I was particularly taken by the curious mixture of development and decay.

There was one decent town with some reasonable shops, while the marina itself had an excellent restaurant next to a place that sold tourist goods and souvenirs. Luckily *Mary Helen* has very little room for such things so I saved a great deal of money! What made it even better was the fact that the marina kindly gave us a 10 percent discount because we'd been stuck there so long.

My youngest son James had been planning to meet us in Bermuda on May 14th but because of the delay we had to put him off for a week.

News bulletins had been reporting severe storms in Bermuda. My father had been caught in one in 1934 (I always said 'served him right!') and when Donald was sailing in *Bluebird* with Lord Riverdale in 1964 they meet a hurricane and were reported as lost. They weren't of course, but merely lying a-hull and waiting until conditions got better. As you might imagine therefore, we were wary of Bermuda and her storms.

Having had enough of West End we decided to move on Thursday, May 10th by which time the wind had abated a little. We would force our way across the Little Bahama Bank, making two overnight stops, before heading for Green Turtle Cay where, nearby, was an exit to the Atlantic.

A large crowd gathered to see us off, and as they slipped out of sight astern, we quickly got down to business, negotiating our way through Indian Passage and out to the Little Bahama Bank. There was very little water, but both boats made it through without touching. With the westerly breeze strengthening, the short seas quickly washed the decks clean, so soon, every trace of marina grime had completely disappeared. We anchored that night off Mangrove Cay.

The following day we pressed on past Great Sale. We were in no mood to hang about so made plenty of use of the engine. It was a hard slog to windward and dusk was falling when we finally anchored at Hawksbill Cay.

Up early the following morning, we left the anchorage at 0900 against an easterly Force 2 – 4. With shelter from the windward Cays the sea was less aggressive than it might have been and we just made it over the bar into White Sound, Green Turtle Cay, with about 3 inches to spare. Ian, aboard *Independent Freedom*, had to anchor outside.

The forecast was optimistic, suggesting lighter winds, perhaps from the north-west.

A gale was expected near Bermuda four days hence, they said. We would pass on that, we decided.

Leaving Green Turtle Cay at 1000, when there was enough water over the bar, we headed south-east towards Whale Cay channel, our exit to the Atlantic. After that, we were homeward bound and heading east.

Headwinds stayed with us for three days, strengthening to a north-easterly Force 6. Nasty seas built up and we shipped a lot of water on board. Then late on the third day, the strong north-easterly died away and by 0400 on the fourth day, we were motoring again.

Slowly during the morning, a breeze emerged from the south-west, strengthening to Force 4 – 5. It was more than welcome and sent *Mary Helen* tramping along at more than 5 knots in the right direction.

After dark, lightning illuminated the heavens. The mainsail was handed in anticipation of a thunderstorm, which duly hit us at midnight to the accompaniment of rain. Luckily there was no wind with this storm, but it was only when the thick clouds cleared away that we felt sufficiently confident to set the mainsail.

The wind was now blowing from the north-east again, but quickly backed to the north and freshened.

We had one more day of calm weather, before a good south-south-west wind sprang up which had *Mary Helen* back on track and sailing quickly. By midnight, we had two reefs in the mainsail and were moving well through a large, but easy sea.

According to our calculations, and provided the wind held up, a landfall the following evening, was just about possible. Everything went according to plan, with *Mary Helen* speeding along at up to 6 knots, but then the breeze fell away, heading us a little, and visibility fell to about 3 miles. At 1600, there, up ahead, was Bermuda. We'd made it without mishap after a challenging sail. An interesting rather than entertaining passage, I decided, but at least nothing had broken and, once again, *Mary Helen* had performed like a thoroughbred. Just then an aeroplane flew over and we wondered if it was James.

After spending the night alongside the Customs Quay at St George's Town, we made our way to Hamilton where Michael, Ian's crew motored out in the dinghy to guide us in. Amazingly, *Independent Freedom* had only beaten us by eight hours!

At the Royal Bermuda Yacht Club marina we also met James who jumped on board and asked for a lift home – and yes, it had indeed been his plane! We spent five days here, much of the time preparing for our crossing to the Azores. By now this was a well established routine – stowing provisions, making lists and ticking everything off.

But it wasn't all work. As it happened, one of James's colleagues happened to be in Bermuda at the time and he showed us round the island and took us to several marvellous restaurants.

Shortly after our arrival, we were also invited to a lecture at the Club by Olin Stephens the famous yacht designer. At 92, he was even older than me but as everyone knows, sailing keeps you young. I was delighted to meet him, not just because of the important role he played in the evolution of modern yachts but because he and John were contemporaries. These were the days of Jack Laurent Giles, John Illingworth and Angus Primrose.

Like many yachtsmen of the period, Olin taught himself to sail – as indeed did his brother Rod. But designing was his passion and at the age of 21, after an apprenticeship with

the great Philip Rhodes, teamed up with a yacht broker
called Drake Sparkman to form one of the most famous
partnerships in yachting history.

He's a great role model, not least because fame came
slowly. After all, the fledgling company was founded in the
teeth of the Great Depression, and it was only when Olin's
father commissioned them to design an ocean racer that
things began to get better. The boat they produced, a yawl
called *Dorade* was full of innovative ideas, and in 1931, won
the seventh Fastnet Race. As they years went by, she was
followed by a succession of Sparkman and Stephens (S&S)
designed boats which not only won subsequent Fastnets,
but ocean races all over the world. When I met Olin at the
Club he was promoting his recent autobiography and was
kind enough to sign my own personal copy.

Talking about the old days and the people we both knew
brought back so many memories. For a start, there was Jack
Laurent Giles, John's best friend. At the time, of course, he
was Britain's leading yacht designer and many of the boats
he designed became classics. In those famous offices at 4
Quay Hill in Lymington, the original partners – George Gill,
Humphrey Barton, and, of course, Jack Laurent Giles himself
– started a minor revolution, the effects of which have been
profound.

One has only to think of boats like *Myth of Malham* and
Gulvain – or the way he popularised light displacement and
canoe-bodied hulls to realise the significance of his
contribution. Jack then, was undeniably ahead of his time.
He was also the first to introduce reverse sheer. The idea
was to create more space amidships, where it was most
needed, and was widely copied. I once joked that it
produced a strange effect; as though the boat had run into a
pier backwards. Suffice it to say he was not amused.

Having said that, he was good fun – but he took his
design work seriously and expected others to do the same.
We're still friends of the family today, and his clergyman son,
has been dubbed 'Tew's Honorary Parson!' My John was his

godfather and James is his godson. Unfortunately we missed his christening as we were stuck on the mud in Poole Harbour! Jack's other son still works as a designer for the American Navy.

I also thought about Eric Hiscock and the time I helped him to get into the R.C.C. He'd written to my father asking for his support, but Dad was away skippering the Grenfell Mission ship in Newfoundland, so I replied instead – and eventually went sailing with him, along with my friend Mollie, in his original *Wanderer*, which was only about the size of a Hillyard two tonner. We had great fun and Mollie ended up trying on Eric's trousers while Eric slipped on Mollie's skirt. In those days it wasn't the done thing for girls to wear trousers so it was all rather daring. Not surprisingly perhaps, she looked much better than he did! Eric, who went on to become a cruising legend actually learnt a great deal from Roger Pinckney in *Dyarchy*, as he mentions in his early books.

Roger was another wonderful character and a superb sailor. He always seemed to assemble a crew of cheerful young people and, in the evenings, some sort of music would usually emanate from *Dyarchy*'s cabin. His mother, Mrs P as she was always known, sailed with him until she was more than 90 and was always in charge of stores etc. She also like to bathe but as she got older, diving overboard, not to mention getting back again, became rather difficult, so Roger organised a bosun's chair which meant he could gently dip her in.

Quite a few of us used to meet up in St Peter Port for an early season scrub (the inner harbour used to dry out then) and I remember sailing over with a school friend. We'd had a fairly breezy passage and poor Norah was extremely seasick.

When she was lying miserably on the lee bunk, Dad tried to make the wireless work to get a forecast, but all he got was whistling and crackling. Norah thought we were about to sink and that Dad was trying to call for help. Truth to tell, she was in such a bad way that she didn't care if we were rescued or not. Predictably, she never came sailing again!

Looking back, I feel incredibly privileged to have known so many of our early pioneering sailors. Meeting Alain Gerbault of *Firecrest* fame was a particularly proud moment. He was the R.C.C. guest at the Commodore's party which celebrated the Club's first 50 years. I'd pin up pictures of him at home, because that wouldn't have been allowed at school then. He also gave me a signed menu.

Then there was the time that Sir Arthur Underhill, who founded the Club, presented me with an R.C.C. broach when Dad won the Challenge Cup for our Færoes cruise. I still wear it with pride. Sir Arthur's boat was called *Wulfruna*. She had a lovely schooner bow and, I recall, she and *Emanuel* became a bit over friendly at a meet in Helford and had to be separated with fenders.

Another luminary was Claud Worth, our Vice-Commodore – one of the early yachting writers. His original *Yacht Cruising* was the definitive cruising and maintenance manual of its time, though it later had several near copies written by other authors. He was an eminent Harley Street eye specialist and he used to tell a lovely tale of how, one rainy day, while walking in Cowes wearing his yachting clothes, a little girl, one of his London patients, spotted him and said, "Oh look Mummy, there's Mr Worth" "Nonsense dear," she replied, " he'd never be seen looking like that!" and quickly walked away.

I'm hugely proud to have signed copies of his two principal books.

Frank Carr who was curator of Greenwich Museum for many years also gave me a signed copy of his *Sailing Barges*. When I was at college, he even took me out to lunch at the House of Lords where he had a temporary job as a librarian. I'm sure I boasted about that to my friends!

In the summer of 1934 when Dad deserted me, I had a super August sailing in *Blue Dragon* with Skipper Lynham on the north coast of Scotland. He was larger than life and the Dragon prep school's leading light.

Skipper, as he was always called, was a true cruising sailor and had been at Oxford with my John's father. John also became a Dragon as did each of our five sons and two of my grandsons.

It's amazing how often you bump into fellow Dragons. We even met one in the West Indies. Skipper used to sail a lot on the west coast of Scotland and *Blue Dragon* was a regular visitor to out of the way anchorages. Rumour has it that one year he was writing up bills for the school, when a gust of wind blew them overboard. He subsequently sent an apologetic letter to the parents, asking them to pay what they thought they owed! He used to do most of the cooking on board in a deep-fry pan. It was best not to ask when the fat had been last changed – but for all that, his concoctions were surprisingly tasty!

I also remember climbing the Skuir of Eigg and going to great pains to get a picture of Duncan (one of the crew) to make it look dangerous. Duncan later married Betty who was also on board and became a high powered diplomat. His son and my Donald were Dragons together and became best friends.

Some time later, as John and I were sailing to Cherbourg one day, we noticed a small boat about the same size as ours which looked vaguely familiar.

"Of course, it's *Lottie Blossom*, Arthur Ransome's latest," says John.

So we sailed close to her and exchanged greetings. Later, we met up again in the Beaulieu River and quickly became friends. I served on the R.C.C. committee with Arthur, and would journey up to London to have tea with the family before going on to the Club.

Naturally, as a sailing family we read all his books and, with a family of my own, I used to read them to the boys at bedtime. They still strike a chord with me; I know exactly how Susan felt in *We Didn't Mean to go to Sea.* I too had felt cold and miserable and sick – on precisely the same passage! Now I belong to the Arthur Ransome Society and also the *Nancy Blackett* Trust. *Nancy* is about the same size as my *Mary Helen*, and flys the R.C.C. burgee! If you don't know what I'm talking about I suggest you quickly beg, borrow, buy or steal any of the Arthur Ransome books. You won't regret it.

It was all most entertaining and, had it been possible, we might have stayed longer – Bermuda was so thriving, busy and friendly, but we wanted to avoid the hurricane season and time was pressing.

Track of *Mary Helen* through the Caribbean

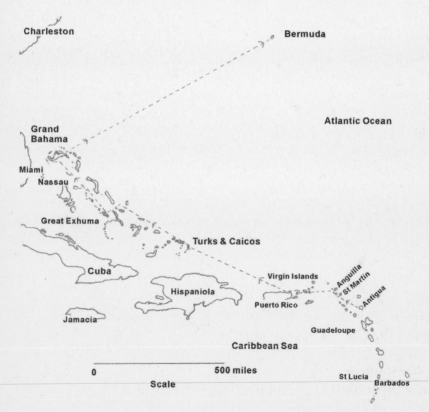

Chapter Thirteen

ARRIVAL BACK - BEAULIEU

On Saturday, May 6th we finally left. It was miserable. The wind of course, was a Force 3, north-east by east, the sky was overcast, and the south channel a trifle lumpy. In the end therefore we went through Ferry Cut to St Georges Harbour, where we anchored for the night.

We left St Georges the following day in a south-easterly Force 5, and a foul sea, under a dark grey sky. With two reefs in the main and the bowsprit plunging into relentless head-on seas we were constantly drenched by showers of spray and progress was slow.

The following day was quite different. We shook out the reefs and the wind died.

The sun even managed a brief appearance – but then the clouds returned, along with a breeze from south-east by south.

This, then was a difficult passage – which is why it was good to have James with us. Most importantly it made watch-keeping considerably easier. With six hours off and only three hours on, it was absolutely luxury!

For the next two days we were hard on the wind, just managing to keep her on course. For the most part it was grey and cloudy, with *Mary Helen* staggering through it.

Our proud little ship was taking quite a bashing which no doubt caused some of the planks to move and the seams to work. Anyway, what with all the spray as well, it was hardly surprising that the bilges filled so quickly. We certainly had to pump quite a lot.

While off watch down below, a particularly violent lurch hurled me against the forward berth and I thought I'd broken my ribs. When James called me to take over from him, I found I could hardly move – so when he offered to take my stint himself, I gratefully accepted. Luckily the injury was slight so I was soon mobile again, and that was the only watch I missed.

On our fourth day out, the wind freed a little and, for a while, the sun shone brightly. What a difference; even the sea looked bluer. We were on course and making 5 knots. James, who earlier, had been suffering from seasickness, was feeling much better and, while it was damp below, the boat wasn't leaking so much.

For the next three days we made good progress. It rained a bit but the wind was fair, first south-westerly then north-west between Force 3 and 4; the ships motions had become easier too. After a couple more days of strong north-westerly winds and clear sunny skies, *Mary Helen* settled down nicely and we enjoyed some really good sailing.

By the evening of Tuesday June 5th however, we watched as heavy rain clouds started building from the west. Then the wind died. Early next morning a south-westerly wind developed and steadily strengthened bringing with it heavy rain. Quickly a vicious sea grew up, along with a heavy cross swell. Steep waves appeared and *Mary Helen* was soon shipping water. Her bowsprit was dipping again as she rose and fell. It was most uncomfortable. By mid day, the wind was blowing from south-south-west, reached Force 7 and stayed there for three days. There was rain and drizzle for good measure and visibility was poor.

By Sunday June 10th conditions improved though it remained cloudy and drizzly. On Monday and Tuesday it blew hard again with nasty breaking cross seas which came splashing on board. Humidity below had risen to just over 90 per cent and there was intermittent rain. Just about everything was damp.

Wednesday June 13th was a complete contrast. The seas had reduced, the wind was a light west-north-westerly and the sun radiated much needed warmth from a clear blue sky. This was out first chance to dry everything out so we opened the forehatch and let the breeze blow through. The motion was easier now and we felt proud of our stout little ship.

As dawn broke on Thursday, we were greeted by a fine north-westerly breeze which gave us a brilliant sail. The sea was moderate and, as we soaked up the sun, we felt quite a sense of satisfaction.

Then, suddenly, it was all over. Predictably, and undramatically, we picked out the outlines of Faial and Pico from some way off and gently made our way in – finally making fast alongside the customs berth at 1130. Formalities completed, they directed us to an excellent spot in Horta marina.

It came as no surprise that *Independent Freedom* had beaten us to it. Ian had arrived the previous Sunday. Still, we'd not done so badly!

After four days which was enough time for a nasty weather front to pass through, *Mary Helen* left Horta behind.

It was a fine sunny day, and though the wind was rather feeble, we noticed a fairly heavy swell breaking on rocks at the north-west end of Sao Jorge. We finally anchored in Vila de Prais, Graciosa where *Mary Helen* rolled around a little – but at least it was quiet.

Just after breakfast on Wednesday June 20th, we left Graciosa in bright sunshine driven along by a decent breeze from west-north-west. We were sailing fast on course for Start Point – and home.

It stayed like that for three days although the wind slowly eased off. Two days later it was dull and overcast with heavy rain which cleared away on the second day. When the sun eventually did come out, we hung our oilskins out to dry. For a while the wind came ahead, north-north-west Force 3, but then settled down to the north-west.

On Tuesday June 26th, dawn broke on a day which saw plenty of sunshine. As the wind slowly backed south-west and freshened, *Mary Helen* found herself running in a moderate sea. For three more days she continued chortling along in much the same way before crossing the continental shelf.

People who don't sail often wonder how we manage to carry enough supplies.

Well, on such a small boat, it's certainly a struggle.

To start with, we have a ten gallon water tank but for this particular ocean voyage we also took various plastic containers, some stowed forward some tucked behind the cabin settee. That meant I lost an area usually reserved for milk and butter. We always used water sparingly and allowed a mere half a mug for teeth cleaning and a wet sponge for face washing. Lucy bought some 'Wet Wipes' which you could rub over your body to freshen yourself up which we found almost invaluable.

On the other hand, we allowed ourselves as much drinking water as we wanted. At the planning stage, our basic principle was to 'think of the quantity you want, then double it'. The other day somebody in one of the yachting magazines, suggested it might be a mistake to over stock with food and water. I couldn't *disagree* more. In a small boat it's impossible to forecast with any accuracy the time your voyage will take. In our case for example, we reckoned it should last about thirty days. In fact it took just under twenty seven days, but when we broke our gooseneck we it might easily take fifty days or more – and so it would have done had the wind played tricks on us. As it was, we made a relatively fast passage, largely because we carried a second second spinnaker pole and an extra headsail and, naturally, because *Mary Helen* is a such very good sea boat.

But when things went wrong, at least we had plenty of food and water!

Tins went in the bilges. It's important mark the contents with indelible ink because when the labels get wet they disintegrate. There's nothing more annoying than opening what you think is a tin of pineapple only to find its baked beans! These days you can get almost anything in tins and the flavours make them far more palatable than 'the tasteless messes' which Claud Worth endured.

There was no space for salt meat and such like, so on passage, almost everything we ate came out of a can. Having said that, we always stocked up with fresh provisions as much as possible along the way, but at sea food quickly deteriorates. Bananas seemed to go off most rapidly but potatoes never lasted long either. We found that apples lasted best, and because oranges were such a bore to peel they went dry long before they were past their best! Pasta keeps, of course, and we carried macaroni and rice, but they needed lots of valuable water for cooking; that's why we liked our packets of presumably, semi-cooked rice which only needed a couple of tablespoons. We also carried dozens of those small variety packs of cereal. Larger packets would take up too much room. Not only that, once opened, their contents would soon get damp and soggy. Ryvita and dried biscuits were used as substitutes for bread, and naturally we had a good stock of Mars Bars, Kit Kats and Penguins etc, which made convenient snacks when conditions were foul. Eggs kept for about three weeks.

As to the meals we ate, a typical day would start with breakfast, which meant coffee with long-life milk, scrambled eggs or cereal or a slice of bread and butter or Ryvita.

Lunch would consist of fruit juice, cheese biscuits, chocolate biscuits and maybe an apple. In the afternoon we had cups of tea of and a piece of cake. Incidentally a good fruit cake in a decent tin will keep for ages as long as you don't eat it all at once.

For supper we might cook one of the rice packets with a tin of meat or fish and vegetables, mixed up rather like a kedgeree. That would be followed by a tin of fruit.

When cruising in colder climates we used to carry stews and soups, but that sort of thing seemed out of place in warmer latitudes.

We also had a 'ready use' locker in the galley with tea, coffee, condiments and spare tins, so you could always get something in a hurry. We cooked on a single small Calor Gaz stove hung in gimbals. I used to have a Primus which I much preferred, but people thought it dangerous. The Calor Gaz stove was a bit awkward to get at, which is one of the reasons I had no compunction in letting Donald do 90 percent of the cooking.

We carried eight gallons of diesel in the tank but lashed another couple of cans to the rigging. I kept calling it petrol because the old Stuart Turner ran on a mixture of petrol and oil – and old habits die hard.

Oilskins were kept in a starboard side locker by the companionway. It was supposed to be a hanging locker but wasn't really big enough. We had to stow oilskins there to keep the saloon seats dry. How I hated putting them on and struggling out of them again. There was another hanging locker forward in which we kept our shore-going clothes on hangers. They stayed dry in there but the boat's motion rubbed a patch in Donald's best jacket! Since there were only two of us, we used the forward berth for stowage too. We also carried a sleeping bag each as well as a blanket in case someone needed wrapping up. We kept the liferaft in the cabin, under the table.

It was horribly in the way but in an emergency there would be no point having it hidden up in the forepeak.

Our table was made of solid teak and very firmly fixed which gave excellent support when you were moving about in rough weather. The top opens out flat for chartwork. John had also made a chart case which was lashed against a locker forward and kept the charts nice and flat. Rolled up charts are a menace!

By Saturday June 30th, the cobalt blue sea had disappeared, to be replaced by the cold, grey waters of the English Channel.

With considerably more ships about, there was plenty to look at – and even the pigeons expressed confidence in us; two stayed with us for twenty four hours. That night it drizzled and the wind died away completely.

Sunday, July 1st dawned dull and cloudy. But then, as we rounded Start Point, with the wind piping up from the north-west, and the sun shining through. *Mary Helen* started accelerating dramatically and was soon racing across the Bay at 7 knots.

We sailed close past Blackpool Sands and once abeam of Stoke Flemming, in view of the church spire, dipped our ensign in memory of John who was buried there.

This was his little boat; his brilliant design, first sketched on the back of a menu, which had taken us safely across the Atlantic and back without once causing any concern, a fitting tribute.

Both my sons know Dartmouth well, so with a touch of bravado, the boys sailed *Mary Helen* between the Dancing Beggars and the mainland, a channel a mere seventy feet wide. I say bravado but of course they knew what they were doing.

All my sons are natural sailors. Ian was only eight when he made his first passage across the Solent in our 11ft sailing Scow. To prove he'd really got there, he went ashore and bought a china ornament with 'a souvenir from Cowes' written on it.

He then developed into a pretty good Firefly sailor and at Pangbourne even rivalled Rodney Pattison, who later went on to win gold medals in the Flying Dutchman class.

Malcolm eventually took over the Firefly but was soon sailing 420s which became the Beaulieu River Sailing Club's principal class. The 420's international status meant we used to go to lots of venues abroad and since the boys were young it meant I had to drive them about and became very involved.

Of course, driving on the wrong side of the road with a dinghy astern took a bit of getting used to, and I remember approaching a huge roundabout in France and being so completely flummoxed that I stopped in the middle. Luckily a friendly French gendarme realised my predicament, stopped all the traffic and put me on the right track. By the time we went to the 'Worlds' in Czechoslovakia I was considerably bolder and, according to James, broke all the speed limits on the German Autobahns. There was nothing cavalier in all this; I merely misunderstood the regulations.

Czechoslovakia was most interesting. Our team failed to win but was well placed. Some of the local boats looked extremely sorry for themselves but their skippers seemed very cheerful and the atmosphere was immensely friendly. I've no doubt that competitions like this are excellent ways of building international friendship and understanding. Having dozens of young people from different parts of the world gathered around a bonfire laughing and singing can do nothing but good.

We even went to Rhode Island in America one year where our team gave me a bright yellow T-shirt with 'Team Mummy' printed across it. That was in the days before sponsorship, of course.

We also sailed *Mary Helen* to several overseas meetings; she was actually the official British HQ at Medemblic in Holland. James came second in the singlehanded class here, so you can imagine the pride of the British team as they sang *God Save the Queen* on the podium. I have to say the cheering was much louder for him than for the chap from another country who came first!

On another occasion Ian and I sailed *Mary Helen* up to Jullynge in Denmark for the 'Worlds'. It's a small place halfway up the Roskilde fjord, and as we sailed in with the 420 flag flying from our crosstrees we were met by one of the 420 Jullynites, who escorted us through the tricky channel to the marina and a specially reserved berth. What a wonderful welcome! The Danes were incredibly friendly and not only took me out on their yachts to watch the racing, but even drove me to Copenhagen where I found (amongst other things) a super embroidery shop!

The British team all finished high up, and everyone thoroughly enjoyed themselves.

In fact Malcolm won quite a few of the British 420 cups and was actually British champion for two years – which gave me immense pride but I tried to keep it under control. Parental onlookers should never show obvious favouritism!

Of course, as the young get older they move on to larger boats and get involved with families and careers but the boys never lost their enthusiasm. The grandchildren don't sail as much as their parents used to but the Tew name is still finding its way on to some of the local trophies

Anyhow, at 1715 we were now back in England, alongside the Royal Dart Yacht Club on our favourite river. I reminded myself that the Tews don't want to go to heaven and sing hymns; their idea of paradise is to go to Dartmouth and fish.

We left Dartmouth as the fog closed in and stayed with us until we reached Portland Bill. Thank heaven for radar – it's such a comfort in conditions like this. We spent the night in Lulworth Cove before cruising across to Yarmouth. Donald got in touch with his family to keep them up to date and I popped ashore to get my hair cut. After all, I wanted to look my best!

The word had obviously spread, and as we left the Isle of Wight on Thursday, July 5th 2001, slipping our mooring in Yarmouth after a night of thunder and lightning, the Lymington lifeboat escorted us back to Beaulieu. A number of other boats including *Sunmaid* owned by Anthony and Sheila Penfold (R.C.C.), *Cygnet of Beaulieu*, along with a helicopter, plus one lone Scow joined us on our way up the

river to the Club pontoon – almost twelve months after we'd
left it.

What a reception awaited me. As I went ashore,
champagne corks popped and people waved and cheered; it
was most bemusing and I was surprised that so many
friends and well wishers had come out to greet me.

"After all" I said, "I only went for a sail!"

EPILOGUE

I was amazed by people's reactions. It never entered my head that I'd done anything unusual, but it would be hypocritical to say that I didn't enjoy it all. People were so kind; I also felt a huge sense of satisfaction when other 'senior citizens' said they'd been inspired. I also received a lot of super letters, some from complete strangers, one from an old school friend, who wondered, "Are you the Helen Graham I was at Poltimore with?" This was the school near Exeter which I went to before Cheltenham. I was even asked to give a short talk there and it was a curious sensation to find oneself standing on the stage of the Princes Hall, gazing out over a sea of faces, rather than sitting in the audience with the children.

Actually I was asked to talk at several clubs and societies which was extremely flattering. It also worked out well for the R.N.L.I. As an amateur I felt it was inappropriate to charge fees, so when people offered I told them a donation to the R.N.L.I. would be appreciated. They were most generous.

Another of my letters was from Ellen MacArthur's 'Nan'. She wrote in a heart-warming way and it was through her that I got in touch with Ellen herself. Of course everyone was talking about her astonishing achievements, so I was both surprised and flattered to be voted runner-up for the 'Yachtswoman of the Year' award. What a contrast! Here was this young, brave, attractive, singlehander who understood all about satellite navigation systems etc, alongside *Mary Helen*'s elderly owner who merely pottered across the 'Pond' with her son!

She was incredibly charming and took the trouble to come across and present me with her bottle of champagne. One day when she's outgrown all this high powered sailing, I hope she'll find time to go cruising and get as much fun as I've had. Cruising gives you the chance to explore some of the more exciting places in the world that you miss when you're racing round the world. Of course, having owned a 21ft Corribee, she knows about small boats too, so I think she'd appreciate *Mary Helen*.

For my part I've never wanted to sail singlehanded, I enjoy the company of other people too much. I also like discussing plans and re-living my adventures with people who were there at the time. Naturally, it's important to have the right company, but I've always been lucky. As my father used to say, "The answer to the crew problem is to breed them". John and I took his advice, and so did Dad himself!

All in all, then, I think cruising keeps you young. But if you want to know the secret of long life – and it's a question I was constantly asked when I returned, I think it's probably luck – though if you keep busy and have plenty of interests you don't think about getting old! I've been lucky in that respect because my John was like-minded and always encouraged me.

I've belonged to our local amateur drama group for ages and instead of objecting to me coming home late after rehearsals he always had a hot meal ready for me! He also loyally supported our plays and supplied some of the props. I remember on one occasion my granddaughter Emily had lent us her favourite cuddly toy, a black pig. While one of the actors was nursing it on stage a shrill little voice from the audience rang out, "Look Daddy; Granny's got my piggy nig." After which nothing was quite the same again.

Over time, of course, there are fewer numbers of parts one can play so I gradually became increasingly involved in production which was absolutely fascinating, but even lately I've had the odd chance to 'tread the boards'. While playing Queen Victoria in her old age I broke my ankle but it didn't matter, I was in a wheel chair anyway! Perhaps appropriately my last performance was as 'Time' in Shakespeare's Winter's Tale. Having started my illustrious acting career as a fairy at the age of seven I think I've just about covered the field.

We also had an excellent drama group at our W.I. People are often disparaging about amateur all-women groups like this but my South Baddersley W.I. were daunted by nothing and our production of Euripides 'Trojan Women' was awarded a gold star; we were also one of the four chosen to perform at County level. It's amazing what you can do if you try. A decent production also demands proper research and I remember going to Chawton to see Jane Austin's house when we were doing a play about her. We also went down to Exmouth to visit Lady Nelson and Emma Hamilton's houses. It made a huge difference.

All told, I've been a W.I. member for over fifty years and gained enormously from it. It offers so much, not least friendship, education and self improvement. You name it, the W.I. does it. I was particularly pleased to see an article about our Atlantic trip in *Home and County*, the W.I. magazine. I felt it reflected something of the get up and go attitude of the organisation.

For me though, sailing has been my life – which is why I never want to stop. Fortunately, there are other people of mature years with similar views.

As a case in point, I remember a few years ago, before the crossing when my good friend Gill Lloyd just about saved my sanity. She and another friend, Liz Bates, were extremely disappointed when their elderly husbands gave up sailing and thought we might organise something together instead.

My *Mary Helen* was laid up, Liz's boat had been sold, but *La Snook*, Gill's sturdy 25ft Fisher, was still in commission so we three grannies, with twenty-five grandchildren between us, decided to have some fun.

Gill and I had both owned 11ft sailing Scows so we weren't entirely rusty.

I sailed more regularly, usually with Beaulieu River Sailing Club, and normally finished last while my sons often led the fleet. I did actually win one race though, largely because the fresh breeze suited my ample weight. In fact, I was fighting a losing battle with one of our better sailors when the wind suddenly hit us just towards the end. I simply needed to hang out a bit more – but she had to spill the wind which slowed her down – so I pipped her to the line! I don't think I've ever have won a race since, but I've still enjoyed myself.

Anyhow, Gill thought it might be a bit of a lark to 'thread the Needles', after all Roger Pinckney had apparently done it in *Dyarchy* which was several times larger.

So, one fine day, when the wind and tide were right, we set off. I sailed from my home on Thorn's Beach and met up with Gill at the mouth of the Lymington River. Successfully managing to stay clear of the Yarmouth/Lymington ferry, we then cruised merrily across the Solent. I think we must have featured in quite a few holiday albums because we saw several cameras pointing in our direction. I suppose people are used to things like racing dinghies and rescue boats but not a couple of white haired old grannies in tiny blue Scows.

As we approached our destination, the cliffs appeared longer and higher, and more menacing. They look super from a safe distance – but it's a different story when you get up close! And then, suddenly, there we were, sailing towards the gaps in the rugged white Needles.

But where was the deepest water? Although the tide was slack, we were still confronted by a mass of bubbling white water and dangerous-looking rocks! We hardened our hearts, held our breath, headed for the least turbulent patch and, lo and behold, slipped effortlessly through!

The Needles looked friendly again from the other side and we burst into song:

" We'll range and we'll rove like true British sailors;
We'll range and we'll rove all on the salt seas;
Until we strike soundings in the channel of England;
From Ushant to Scilly is thirty-five leagues."

We sailed across Scratchell's Bay, hauled our boats up the beach and went for a swim. We had the world to ourselves, there was no need to worry about bathing costumes and we felt happy and relaxed, until up on the cliff we saw some hikers with glasses!

We had towels, but anyway, why worry!

The voyage back was equally satisfying especially when we found an eddy close inshore and completely outsailed a much larger sailing cruiser.

After that, we felt ready to take *La Snook* down to the West County for the R.C.C. meet. So, at the beginning of June, having watched a lovely easterly wind blow to waste, off we sailed from the Royal Lymington Yacht Club early one Sunday morning. We reached Weymouth after a couple of tacks where we met up with friends which was most enjoyable, even though they brought us bad news. Apparently a Force 7 had been forecast for the following day. But next morning's, broadcast suggested much lighter winds – Force 3 – 4 – so we set off at 0800 to catch the tide at Portland Bill. This is where it gets dramatic. The wind freshened as we approached the Bill and a tear appeared in the leech of the working jib.

I'm the resident seamstress on board, so down it came and up went the genny, whilst I repaired the split and we re-set it. Unfortunately in the general rush, the jib halyard hadn't been properly attached so, as Liz hauled it up, it came adrift and fluttered tantalisingly out of reach. There was a lively motion and it soon became obvious that we needed smoother water to sort it all out. In the end, we anchored in the quiet of Balaclava Bay just outside Portland Harbour.

As Skipper, Gill insisted on being the one to go aloft, so with considerable hilarity, Liz and I used the main halyard and anchor winch to hoist her up to the masthead. All went well and our troubles were over.

We sped back to the Bill with a strong ebb tide and a foul lumpy race about a mile offshore and were soon in the more stable waters of West Bay, where we streamed the log and set a westerly course.

Then Gill went below. Calamity! The cabin was full of fumes, so we turned the engine off as Gill emerged gasping for air!

We now had the prospect of a long beat, but the sun was out and visibility good, and we made good progress, eventually getting as far as Sidmouth, by which time the tide had turned.

On the seaward tack we were making no headway at all, so with much trepidation we decided to try the engine again. It started, but was still belching out foul black smoke. Gill thought we should try running it for an hour. Liz and I held our breath and tried to work out a way of getting Gill out from the cabin if the fumes overwhelmed her.

All went well and by midnight we reached Torquay tying up alongside a large swishy motorboat in the marina. A rather sleepy owner emerged and was ready to blow his top, but seeing we obviously knew what we were doing, quickly mellowed and told us about his hard day's slog across the bay. When we told him we'd just done the same his attitude changed completely. In the end, we found him both helpful and friendly.

Next day we had an excellent sail round to Dartmouth, La Snook skimming along like a bird in the fresh squally breeze. Arriving at Dartmouth was a bit of an anticlimax; there was no sign of any R.C.C. yachts at all. However, after a tot of rum and some grub, we spotted the fleet further up the river. They gave us a terrific welcome; after all, we were the smallest vessel there and several bigger boats had thought the weather too inclement.

We slipped around to Salcombe and met up with Liz's family which was fun, then sailed home via Brixham and Lulworth where we spent a lovely quiet evening. We were woken the following morning by the patrol boat. The skipper told us they were firing that day so we couldn't move until the afternoon, but they did give us permission to use their buoy at Chapman's Pool which we thought was very considerate.

Spending another night in Poole was most nostalgic and I expect I bored the other two with my long rambling memories. Then it was back to Lymington in time for roast beef and Yorkshire pud at the Yacht Club. It had all been such fun and so good natured. We spent numerous evenings playing Scrabble and never once had an argument!

That particular adventure set the scene for more granny cruises until 1999 when I got *Mary Helen* back. We visited the Breton coast and explored several new harbours; *La Snook* only draws 3½ft, which meant we could get in much closer than usual.

The most southern port we reached was Merion, opposite Belle Isle, where Gill's family were staying. We even got a mention in the French newspapers here. They called us 'les loups de la mer'.

Then, one year, we went up the Seine to Paris.

We sailed across to Le Harve from Langstone Harbour, where we unstepped the mast and the Yacht Club kindly stored it, along with the sails etc, until we came back.

It was a bit disconcerting turning the yacht into a motor boat but we gradually got used to it.

We were joined by our good friend Claude de Fontenay, a retired Seine pilot who once piloted the Queen up the river in *Britannia* – and guided us through the Seine's maze of estuary bays. Since he was used to big ships he found *La Snook*'s freeboard a bit on the low side! Either way, having him on board and listening to his reminiscences, was a great bonus and much appreciated.

We just caught the tide for Rouen but were too late for Claude's train to Paris.

"Never mind, you can spend the night on board," we suggested.

He seemed doubtful, but after Liz's super supper and a couple of bottles of wines, provided by Claude himself, he relaxed completely and we enjoyed a peaceful evening admiring the beautiful floodlit cathedral.

Fortified by a proper English breakfast, Claude caught the train to Paris the following morning while we continued up river to the tideless stretch of the Seine. Winding its way through attractive countryside past picturesque towns and villages, the river was fascinating and full of surprises. Even the engine seemed remarkably quiet and smooth. The sun was out too!

We spent a night at Les Andeleys where Richard Cœur de Lion's castle dominated the scenery and primed the imagination. What tales it could tell!

This is where we met *Idle Pursuit*, a comfortable 35ft motor cruiser, whose considerably greater speed meant her thoughtful owners could arrive ahead of us, find suitable mooring places and be ready to take our lines. We had a wonderful time with them.

On the Sunday the river banks were alive with holiday makers and masses of small boats. The French certainly know how to enjoy themselves!

And then, what a thrill; there ahead of us was the Eiffel Tower. So the river really did go to Paris! It had been a fairly long passage but was well worth it.

We eventually found ourselves right in the centre of Paris in the Port de Plaisance, a few minutes walk from the Place de La Bastille and surrounded by rose gardens.

We spent several lazy days here socialising with Gill's friends, and even had lunch at the Yacht Club de France, which meant wearing our best clothes and skirts.

In the evening we played Scrabble in the cockpit by the light of candle lanterns, much to the amusement of people on the nearby bridge. They probably saw us as typically mad British.

Then it was back down the river, calling at Monet's garden at Giverny, which is not to be missed. However I have to say it was extremely crowded and packed with Japanese tourists and school children.

At one little marina we lay close to a large motor yacht, whose owner eventually surfaced and commented haughtily,

"I didn't know the R.C.C. had lady members".

Having been a member since 1934, I was struck speechless (a rare occurrence) and spent the rest of the day trying to think of all the sarcastic things I might have said!

Back in Le Harve we were re-united with our mast and sails and set off along the Normandy coast. We anchored at Arromances at low water with many of the old caissons still visible. Ashore there were masses of buses and people visiting the museum, so we stayed on board and drank a toast to Gill's husband Dick and all the other brave soldiers and sailors who'd landed there fifty years earlier.

Somehow it all seemed a bit too eerie so we upped anchor and motored round to Port-en-Bessin.

We spent a night in St Vaast and met up with *Idle Pursuit* again and had a wonderful time. Then we sailed back to Lymington, still laughing and enjoyed a final game of Scrabble.

In 1997 the R.C.C. meet was to be held at Carteret. This was a new port for all three of us and a chance not to be missed, so off we went across to Cherbourg with a new toy, a Magellan GPS which we christened 'Maggie'. We still had the old Walker log in case something went wrong but Maggie was beautifully behaved.

Then we had a rather foul, cold sail to Alderney, but soon revived after an excellent dinner at the 'First and Last' where we made friends with a boat load of ancient sailors. We ended up being taken for a drink at the 'Divers' pub by the younger members. Clearly, there was life in the old girls yet!

Our passage down to St Peter Port via the Swinge was wet and cold but we managed to get over the sill into the marina. Once again, I expect I bored them with my reminiscences; a lot has changed since the early 30s when, along with other R.C.C. boats, we used to come over for scrubbing at Easter.

After a few days pottering round Jersey, Chausey and Granville, we finally reached Carteret. As usual the meet was tremendous fun and we met up with lots of old friends. And once again, as the smallest boat in the fleet, we got VIP treatment!

And that really sums it all up. You don't need a lot of money or a huge yacht to enjoy sailing – and, of course, you don't even have to be young.

And as for achieving personal goals, it might be a tired old cliché to say 'it's never too late' but that doesn't mean it's not true.

I think I've just about proved it.

Appendix I

MARY HELEN – THE BOAT

A proper little ship, *Mary Helen* has something of the traditional working boat about her. Unlike today's cruisers, with their cutaway underbodies, her long keel promotes excellent directional stability; it also spreads the ballast out, which dampens the motion in a seaway. On the debit side, modern, light displacement boats might be faster to windward but, in spite of her weight and lack of overhangs, she's certainly no sluggard. One of the reasons for that is her 'clean run aft'; just look at the way the buttock lines sweep dramatically up to the transom leaving firm bilges and a streamlined afterbody.

Clearly, this is a boat designed to crack on even when the weather turns nasty.

To complement such powerful lines, John added a generous gaff rig. Of course, tall, triangular mainsails may be marginally more efficient on a beat but they lose a great deal of drive off the wind and while *Mary Helen* sails well on all points, her performance on a run is nothing short of outstanding. With a topsail and two headsails, her rig is also extremely flexible and splits up the total amount of sail into easily handled areas.

Looking at her lines again, it's hardly surprising that she heaves-to quietly – which, in my book, is extremely important. You simply back the headsail, lash the tiller to leeward and she stops almost dead in her tracks. As I say, having a boat that settles down quickly, without paying off on one tack or the other is extremely reassuring particularly in heavy weather. That's why John gave her a decent forefoot and plenty of grip. He also wanted a boat that was both stiff and easy to steer and *Mary Helen* is very light on the tiller.

She was designed at a time when T. Harrison Butler's theories about hull balance in general and his metacentric shelf theory in particular were the subject of much heated debate. Either way, *Mary Helen* handles delightfully so John obviously got his sums right.

Interestingly, perhaps, *Mary Helen*'s widest point is forward of amidships which gives her what old-timers referred to as a 'cod's head and mackerel tail' appearance which at slow speeds reduces resistance through the water. Modern, stripped-out ocean racers are more wedge-shaped but they also go a lot faster!

As you can see, *Mary Helen* has raised topsides to provide as much space down below as possible. I also think it makes her look a lot sleeker.

The cockpit is relatively small by today's standards – but that's a safety factor. If a big cockpit gets swamped, the extra weight can drag the stern down. Even one with drains takes time to empty. Similarly, the accommodation is modest with only three berths – but John designed the boat for us – and it proved perfectly adequate. As Eric Hiscock wrote in *Cruising Under Sail*:

"For more than a year, the Tews lived aboard, and when visiting them, I found they were extremely comfortable and content. When all without was buried in snow and a bitter north-east wind whistled in the rigging, the little saloon with its red cushions, soft lamplight, and roaring bogie stove, was as snug and comfortable a home as anyone could wish to have."

For the record, *Mary Helen* measures 26.4ft LOA, 23.4ft LWL, with 8.2ft beam and 4.7ft draft. Sail area is 462 sq ft. – and she carries an 18bhp Yanmar diesel driving an offset, three-bladed propeller.

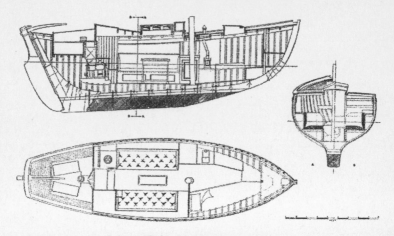

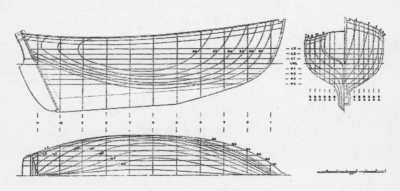

Mary Helen's Accommodation

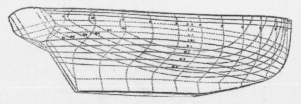

Lines of *Mary Helen*
The upper drawing is the profile or body plan; the lower drawing is
the half-breadth plan, and the right-hand drawing the body plan or
sections

Isometric drawing of *Mary Helen*
1-11: sections. L1-L3: level lines. W1-W4: waterlines.
B1-B6: bow and buttock lines. L.W.L.: load waterline

Appendix II

THE PASSAGE – FACTS AND FIGURES

Time			Passage	Dist-ance	Engine use	
Days	Hrs	Mins		Miles	Hrs	Mins
		30	Beaulieu (Bucklers Hard) to Needs Ore	1.5		30
	7		Needs Ore to Studland	22	2	
5	15		Studland to Camariñas, Spain	547	26	
	10		Camariñas to Portosin	44	10	
	8		Portosin to Sangenjo	37	8	
	6	30	Sangenjo to Bayona	21	6	30
1	12	45	Bayona to Leixoes, Portugal	55	6	30
1	9	45	Lexicoes to Cascais	164	13	
	11	30	Cascais to Sines	53	11	30
	14	15	Sines to Lagos	74	11	30
4	22		Lagos to Porto Santo	453	8	15
3	4		Porto Santo to Lanzarote	322	1	30
	2	15	Porto Calero to Papagayo	7		15
1	14		Papagayo to San Sebastian, La Gomera	184	5	15
26	23	50	La Gomera to English Harbour, Antigua	2700	5	
	4	30	English Harbour to Jolly Harbour	13		30
	1	30	Jolly Harbour to Deep Bay	4		15
	1	45	Deep Bay to Jolly Harbour	4		
	23	40	Jolly Bay to Simpson Bay, St Martin	91	10	30
	4		Simpson Bay to Grand Case	13		15
	3	30	Grand Case to Tintamarre Island	10		15
	7	30	Tintamarre to Marigot Bay, St Martin	25	1	
	1		Marigot Bay to Friars Bay	2.5	1	
	1		Friars Bay to Marigot Bay	2.5		45
	3	30	Marigot Bay to Road Bay, Anquilla	13		15
	6		Road Bay, Seal Island Reef, Prickly Cays, Road Bay	18		5
	19	5	Road Bay to Virgin Gorda Yacht Harbour	75	2	45
	3	50	Virgin Gorda Yacht Harbour to Anegada	18		30
	2	30	Anegada to Prickly Pear Island, Gorda Sound	14		30
		30	Prickly Pear to Biras Creek, Gorda Sound	1		30
	2	30	Biras Creek to The Baths, Virgin Gorda	8		30
	1		The Baths to Marina Cay	5		20
	2	40	Marina Cay to Buck Island	8		45
	1	50	Buck Island to Nanny Cay Marina, Tortola	5		30
	3	50	Nanny Cay to Diamond Cay, Jost Van Dyke Island	12.5		20
	1	10	Diamond Cay to Great Bay	3.25		20
	2		Great Bay to Cruz Bay, St Johns	6.5	2	

	1		Cruz Bay to Fish Bay	4.5		10
	6	15	Fish Bay to Coral Harbour to Fish Bay	20.25		
	3	30	Fish bay to Charlotte Amalie, St Thomas	10.75		30
	1		Charlotte Amalie to Flamingo Bay, Water Island	3.5	1	
	5	40	Flamingo Bay to Ensenada Honda, Isle de Culebra	19	1	15
	5		Isla de Culebra to Isla Palominos	18.5		30
	7	58	Isla de Palominos to San Juan, Puerto Rico	36.25	1	15
3	7	15	San Juan to Cockburn Harbour, South Caicos	380	26	
	1	45	Cockburn Harbour to Six Hills Cays, Caicos Bank	7		30
	6	40	Six Hills Cays to French Cay	33.5		30
	2	45	French Cay to Sapodilla Bay, Providencials	15		20
	2	3	Sapodilla Bay to Georgetown, Great Exhuma	247	29	
		50	Georgetown to Redshank Cays	4.5		50
1	7	45	Redshank Cays to Allan Cay	108.5	20	30
	8	40	Allan Cay to Nassau	37	8	40
	6	53	Nassau to Bird Island, Berry Islands	30.5	6	53
	1	30	Bird Island to Chub Cay	4.5		
	3	45	Chub Cay to Morgans Bluff, Andros	15.5		15
	8	5	Morgans Bluff to Frozen Cay	33		15
		30	Frozen Cay to Little Harbour Cay	1		30
	6	30	Little Harbour Cay to Goat Cay	24	1	30
	4		Goat Cay to Great Harbour Cay Marina	13	1	30
1	1	15	Great Harbour Cay to West End, Grand Bahama	93	2	
	7	45	West End to Mangrove Cay, Grand Bahama Bank	27.75	6	
	12	50	Mangrove Cay to Hawksbill Cay	54	12	50
	6	50	Hawksbill Cay to Green Turtle Cay	32.25	6	50
7	8		Green Turtle Cay to St George's Town, Bermuda	759	77	35
	3		St George's Town to Hamilton	16	3	
	3	45	Hamilton to St George's Harbour	13	3	35
18	4	30	St George's Harbour to Horta, Faial	1753	72	15
	11	40	Horta to Vila da Praia, Graciosa	46	8	30
11	6	20	Vila da Praia to Dartmouth	1214	62	30
	10	5	Dartmouth to Lulworth Cove	56	10	5
	6	25	Lulworth Cove to Yarmouth	31	6	25
	3		Yarmouth to Beaulieu	8		15

Total Time At Sea: 99 days, 14 hours, 39 minutes
Total Engine Time: 21 days, 5 hours, 48 minutes
Total Distance Sailed: 10,246 miles
Average: 103 miles per day
Average Speed: 4.29 knots

Track of *Mary Helen* 2000–2001
UK – Caribbean – UK
Part 1

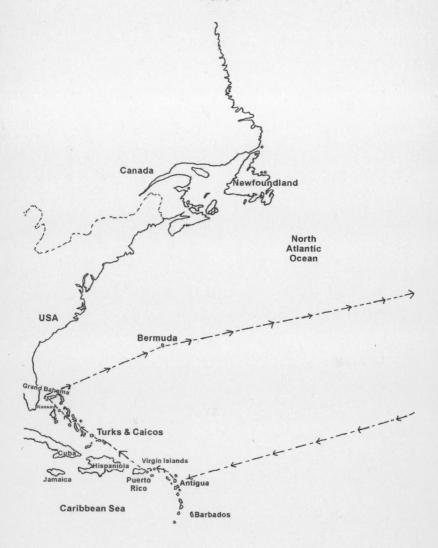

Track of *Mary Helen* 2000–2001
UK – Caribbean – UK
Part 2

ABOUT THE AUTHOR

Born 10 January 1912 – three months before the *Titanic* sank. Educated at Cheltenham Ladies College & Bedford College, London University. Became maths mistress at Leeson School, Swanage. Asked to play cricket for Hampshire but got married instead to John Tew, naval architect in 1936! First Lady to win the Royal Cruising Club Challenge Cup. Helen has five sons and eleven grandchildren. Was President of the British 420s when the boys were leading 420 sailors visiting many countries including the USA. Other interests include R.N.L.I., Cricket, Drama and W.I. Helen has been cruising in small traditional yachts for 81 years.